OVERVIEW

Overview

What ultimately determines the performance of an organization is the behavior of the people that make up that organization. It depends on what individual employees do, and on how they relate to and interact with one another.

So to help ensure an organization's business success, you can focus on promoting the types of individual behavior that will result in the achievement of the organization's goals. Before you can do this though, you need to understand the factors that influence individual behavior, perceptions, and attitudes.

To manage performance effectively, you need to start by recognizing that each employee is a person with a unique background and set of characteristics.

For example, employees' particular personality traits affect the ways they perform and interact with others in the workplace.

If you're familiar with these personality traits, it makes it easier to match employees to the right jobs and tasks. In

1

turn, this can help employees perform to the best of their abilities and contribute to the overall success of your organization.

The ways employees perceive their work and organization typically affect their behavior. Positive perceptions generally lead to greater motivation. And when people are motivated, it's easier to engage them actively at work. So it's important for managers to pay close attention to their individual employees' perceptions and know what factors trigger certain perceptions.

Like perceptions, employees' attitudes to their work can have a dramatic effect on their job satisfaction and performance. Understanding the factors that affect individuals' attitudes is the first step in changing these attitudes.

In this course, you'll learn how understanding organizational behavior can benefit you and your organization. You'll also learn more about the personality traits that affect individual behavior, and about what affects individual perceptions and attitudes.

Understanding what drives individual behavior and how this affects performance in the workplace will equip you to manage employee performance better in your organization.

Organizations don't depend just on the work their employees do in isolation. They also depend on employees working together, interacting and combining their efforts in ways that support high-level business strategies and goals.

Effective collaboration and good group work are critical to an organization's success. So it's important to know what makes a group successful and to do what you can to remove any obstacles that prevent it from performing optimally.

In this course, you'll learn more about what a group is in the context of an organization, and about the internal and external factors that may affect group performance.

You'll learn why it's beneficial to understand group dynamics and the factors that affect group performance.

And you'll learn about the characteristics of effective groups.

For a group to be successful, it has to have the commitment of all its members and support from others, including management. And all group members need enough time to focus on their roles as part of the group, rather than other tasks taking up their time. So as well as learning about groups generally, you'll learn how to overcome resistance to the group and to collaboration, and how to resolve situations where group members have conflicting priorities.

Another important issue to address as part of managing group performance is conflict. In any group situation, some conflict is inevitable. But failing to manage negative types of conflict can prevent people from working together effectively, or at all.

So in this course, you'll learn about typical causes of group conflict. You'll also learn how to address group conflict, using a clear sequence of steps.

Once you've completed this course, you'll be better equipped to promote healthy group interactions and to optimize the performance of groups. In this way, you'll contribute to the success of your organization as a whole.

What's the first thought that pops into your mind when you hear the words organizational politics? Swimming in a tank with sharks? Watching your back?

Unfortunately, these reactions are often justified. Most people have experienced the ugly side of company politics at one point or another in their careers.

However, this isn't the only side to office politics. Healthy and constructive organizational politics is about building relationships that make it possible to align people's efforts and get things done more efficiently.

In this course, you'll learn about the potential benefits of adopting a political mindset at work and about the different types of power that people exert in the workplace. This can help make you more aware of the political landscape in your organization and enable you to navigate it in positive ways.

You'll also learn about the differences between positive and negative political behaviors in an organization, and review examples of these behaviors.

And you'll learn about the characteristic activities of politically constructive leaders in organizations.

Finally, you'll learn about specific political tactics that leaders can use to promote particular courses of action and to get the best from employees in an organization.

Once you've completed this course, you'll be better able to leverage organizational politics. This can help you achieve objectives – your own and those of your organization.

You'll also be able to use your understanding of organizational politics to become a better leader.

Ask yourself why some businesses seem to have an unblemished record of success, while others fight an uphill battle just to break even. Every organization has a structure – the way in which jobs are divided and allocated to staff, and who is in charge. This structure has to suit the organization's needs if it's to succeed. Since many structures haphazardly develop over time, it may be necessary to implement organizational design to push your organization's structure in the right direction.

Successful organizations usually have a solid and stable organizational structure, and implement organizational design wisely.

A solid organizational structure means an organization is always ready to respond to both threats and opportunities, and that it works efficiently as a matter of course.

A clearly defined structure also ensures that employees understand the purpose of their jobs and how they tie in with organizational goals. This tends to make employees more motivated and more efficient.

Using the structure you have effectively – and ensuring that employees adapt to it – can have several benefits. It can lead to better financial performance, better customer satisfaction, and – most importantly – positive employee behavior that supports organizational success.

In this course, you'll learn about different types of organizational structures, the elements that define them, and their advantages and disadvantages.

You'll learn how managers can help employees adapt to the existing structures of their organizations.

And you'll find out about the benefits of redesigning jobs and methods for doing this.

This course will equip you to assess your organization's structure, to help employees perform at their best within that structure, and – when appropriate – to make structural changes. Ultimately, it will help you improve your organization's success, and the motivation and job satisfaction of its employees.

Ask yourself why some businesses seem to have an unblemished record of success, while others fight an uphill battle just to break even. Every organization has a structure – the way in which jobs are divided and allocated to staff, and who is in charge. This structure has to suit the organization's needs if it's to succeed. Since many structures haphazardly develop over time, it may be necessary to implement organizational design to push your organization's structure in the right direction.

Successful organizations usually have a solid and stable organizational structure, and implement organizational design wisely.

A solid organizational structure means an organization is always ready to respond to both threats and opportunities, and that it works efficiently as a matter of course.

A clearly defined structure also ensures that employees understand the purpose of their jobs and how they tie in with organizational goals. This tends to make employees more motivated and more efficient.

Using the structure you have effectively – and ensuring that employees adapt to it – can have several benefits. It can lead to better financial performance, better customer satisfaction, and – most importantly – positive employee behavior that supports organizational success.

In this course, you'll learn about different types of organizational structures, the elements that define them, and their advantages and disadvantages.

You'll learn how managers can help employees adapt to the existing structures of their organizations.

And you'll find out about the benefits of redesigning jobs and methods for doing this.

This course will equip you to assess your organization's structure, to help employees perform at their best within that structure, and – when appropriate – to make structural changes. Ultimately, it will help you improve your organization's success, and the motivation and job satisfaction of its employees.

Organizational culture – sometimes called corporate culture – reflects the beliefs, norms, experiences, and attitudes that prevail in an organization. Every organization has its own culture. Some are strong, positive, and productive. Others are negative and disruptive.

The prevailing culture of an organization influences its members' behaviors, decisions, and corporate values. For this reason, developing a positive culture is a vital step in ensuring an organization's success.

This course describes how to build a positive culture among the people who work in an organization. When employees feel valued by their organization, they're happy, loyal, and motivated to perform well.

This contributes to a pleasant working environment where employees thrive personally and the organization flourishes as a whole.

In this course, you'll find out how to develop an environment in which a positive organizational culture can exist:

- discover the characteristics of a positive organizational culture,
- analyze the drivers of organizational culture, and
- learn strategies for actively cultivating and maintaining a positive organizational culture.

CHAPTER 1 - Organizational Behavior

CHAPTER 1 - Organizational Behavior

Section 1 - The Importance of Organizational Behavior

Section 1 - The Importance of Organizational Behavior

Organizational behavior is the study of human behavior – including individual and group behavior – and its impact on an organization.

Learning about organizational behavior can help you develop a better work-related understanding of yourself and others, and expand your potential for career success. It can help your organization thrive by maximizing productivity and job satisfaction, help you manage human resources more effectively, and help you understand your own work behavior and needs better. It can also help your organization meet the challenges associated with the modern business environment.

Defining organizational behavior

Modern organizations have to be highly efficient, flexible, and productive if they're to survive, or they risk losing out to more dynamic competitors. But why do organizations today have to fight harder to gain and keep a competitive edge?

Modern organizations face various challenges:

- globalization and rapid global communication through technologies like the Internet, resulting in increased competition,
- the increased diversity of workforces, which makes it necessary to manage differences to achieve cohesion and support goals,
- human resource management challenges associated with modern trends, including a shift toward the use of smaller, more flexible, virtual

teams and increased use of strategies like outsourcing, and

- changing attitudes about the employer-employee relationship, including a greater focus on the need for work-life balance.

What's common to each of the challenges facing modern organizations is that they relate to the ways people behave and interact with one another. The study of organizational behavior can help organizations tackle modern challenges. This is because, as a field of study, it investigates the impact of individual and group behaviors on an organization.

Organizational behaviorists divide human behavior into three levels:

- the individual, with behavior driven by personal characteristics and attitudes,
- the group, with members who have to be able to communicate and coordinate their activities to achieve common goals, and
- the organization, whose overall behavior affects its employees and is, in turn, affected by the environment in which it operates.

Note that groups are not the same as teams. A group may be the IT Department or all lawyers working for a multinational company. All the people in a group have their own responsibilities, but a manager typically steers their efforts toward a common goal.

Teams work on single, short-term projects. Everyone participates in shaping the team's goal, under the direction of a team leader. They then work on individual tasks, communicating the results to the team.

Question

Which is the correct definition of organizational behavior?

Options:

1. The behavior of organizations in an international context

2. The study of the impact of individual and group behaviors on an organization

3. A method for ensuring all employees are treated in the same way

4. A type of behavior that illustrates an employee's commitment to an organization

Answer

Option 1: This is an incorrect option. The field of organizational behavior seeks to understand the impact of individual and group behaviors on an organization. It doesn't deal with the behavior of organizations.

Option 2: This is the correct option. The field of organizational behavior studies the effects of individual and group behaviors on organizations.

Option 3: This option is incorrect. Organizational behavior isn't a method for ensuring employees are treated equally. However, understanding organizational behavior – or the impact of human behavior on organizations – can help companies manage diverse workforces.

Option 4: This option is incorrect. The field of organizational behavior studies the impact of individual and group behaviors on an organization. Organizational behavior doesn't refer only to a specific type of behavior by individual employees.

Learning about organizational behavior

Learning about organizational behavior can help you establish how individuals, groups, and your organization as a whole can work together to achieve results in a competitive and dynamic environment.

Specifically, learning about organizational behavior can have several benefits:

- it can help you develop a better work-related understanding of yourself and others,
- it can expand your potential for career success in the dynamic, shifting, and complex new workplaces of today – and tomorrow,
- it helps your organization thrive because it can maximize productivity and job satisfaction,
- it helps you manage human resources more effectively,

- it helps you understand your own work behavior and needs better, thereby maximizing your own satisfaction and productivity, and
- it helps your organization meet the challenges of modern business.

Being aware of organizational behavior helps you understand how the work you do as an individual, and as a member of a group, affects your organization as a whole. Knowing why the work you're assigned is necessary can ensure you work more efficiently. It can also help motivate you.

With this understanding, you can adapt your behavior at work so it's more in line with what you want to achieve. So you can pursue your career goals in a more focused way. You can also take steps to maximize your own job satisfaction, and increase your productivity.

Understanding the behavior of individuals and groups, and how this behavior affects the organization, can help you manage human resources better at all levels.

With a better understanding of yourself and others, you'll get to know why you and your colleagues – as individuals – behave in a certain way at work and what your needs are.

For an organization, better performance by individuals and groups translates into greater success, making it easier to overcome the challenges associated with a competitive, rapidly changing business environment.

Question

What can learning about organizational behavior help you and your organization do?

Options:

1. Understand your own work behavior and needs

2. Develop your career

3. Manage human resources more effectively

4. Overcome business challenges

5. Predict changing business trends

6. Avoid or minimize competition

7. Maximize productivity and job satisfaction

8. Develop a better work-related understanding of yourself and others

Answer

Option 1: This is a correct option. One aspect of understanding organizational behavior is understanding why individuals behave as they do and how this affects their work. This can equip you with a better understanding of your own work behavior and needs.

Option 2: This is a correct option. If you understand your work behavior and how it can affect your organization, you're in a better position to adjust your behavior so that you can achieve specific career goals.

Option 3: This option is correct. Understanding individual and group behavior in an organization can help you manage human resources better.

Option 4: This is a correct option. Understanding organizational behavior can help you manage human resources better and therefore help your organization overcome challenges associated with a rapidly changing, competitive business environment.

Option 5: This is an incorrect option. Understanding organizational behavior can't help you predict trends, although it can equip an organization to respond effectively to change.

Option 6: This option is incorrect. Learning about organizational behavior won't reduce the need for an organization to remain competitive.

Option 7: This is a correct option. Understanding organizational behavior can equip you to improve your own job satisfaction and productivity at work. This will have a positive effect on the organization as a whole.

Option 8: This option is correct. Understanding organizational behavior can result in a better understanding of the work you do and how it fits into the organization. This allows you to work more efficiently.

Section 2 - Factors Influencing Individual Behavior

Section 2 - Factors Influencing Individual Behavior

A variety of characteristics affect individual behavior in the workplace. These include biographical characteristics – generally listed in employees' resumes, natural abilities, and personality traits. Among the main personality traits that affect employee performance – and suitability for particular roles – are extroversion, agreeableness, conscientiousness, emotional stability, and openness to experience.

Individual differences

Organizations are made up of individuals who are unique and behave differently. They have a variety of strengths and weaknesses that will affect their performance at work. Effective human resource management depends on knowing the strengths and weaknesses of employees and managing them accordingly.

If an organization is to meet its business goals, it's crucial that the right people are matched to the jobs that need to be done. In other words, it's important to create the best possible fit between employees and the jobs they're assigned. To do this effectively, you need to understand all the variables that affect individual behavior and performance. Each employee may perform and behave differently in a given situation because of the traits that make that person unique.

Individual differences can be divided into three main categories - biographical characteristics, ability characteristics, and personality traits.

However, these categories aren't static or independent of one another. They interact to make people who they are, working in combination to govern their behavior and responses to given situations.

So they work together to create individual behavioral tendencies, which you can identify and use as the basis for future predictions about individual performance.

Examples of biographical characteristics that can influence people's behavior in the workplace include age and marital status. A person's education and experience can also influence individual behavior. These are the types of characteristics you can usually read from employees' resumes.

Age

Employees approaching an age when they start considering retirement might be less inclined to call in sick or take leave. They're looking forward to retirement but appreciate the last moments of collegial friendship.

Marital status

An employee who is married and also a parent of preschool children might want to work only in an environment that offers flexible time schedules and telecommuting in order to accommodate family responsibilities. On the other side, maybe the employee would want increased responsibilities to make the job more valuable, important, and secure for family responsibilities.

Education

Employees with a high level of education might feel they deserve more flexibility or more rewards because of their contributions and value to the company. Also, they may feel undervalued if they receive tasks that someone with less education could do.

Experience

Your company hires someone who was unemployed for some time. Because of the negative experience of unemployment, he's fearful of losing his job again. He takes on additional responsibilities and tasks only to make himself indispensable to the company. You, as the manager, should recognize this fact and manage the situation accordingly.

Employees' performance doesn't depend just on what education and experience they've had. It also depends on their natural abilities, and on how those abilities are used. Employees who are assigned tasks requiring skills that fall outside their natural abilities usually respond negatively. They perform worse and are likely to become frustrated. So it's important to take employees' abilities into account when managing their performance.

Competencies in three main areas contribute to a person's abilities:

- physical fitness, strength, and coordination,
- intellectual capacity, including the ability to understand complex ideas, adapt to the environment, learn from experience, and engage in various forms of reasoning, and
- emotional skills, including the ability to deal with stress and to demonstrate sensitivity toward others.

All employees are likely to be happier and to perform better if their jobs draw on their natural abilities. For example, only someone who's physically fit and strong will perform well in a job that requires a certain degree of physical ability, like fire-fighting.

Similarly, a person who's naturally good at evaluating information and solving problems is likely to do well and be happy performing those tasks. Someone who doesn't have those natural abilities is less likely to perform well, irrespective of how much training that person completes.

Good emotional abilities may make someone suited to a job in the health care sector for example. The same person may become frustrated in a desk job that doesn't involve relating to others.

People's biographical characteristics and natural abilities are fairly basic traits that play a role in an individual's behavior. However, they're not necessarily fixed.

For example, people age and acquire new experiences. They may also acquire new abilities or uncover abilities they weren't aware they had.

For instance, it's possible to develop your intellectual capacity over time through education and practice.

Personality traits and performance

In contrast, personality traits tend to be constants. They determine intrinsic differences that remain fairly stable throughout people's lives. Five important personality traits that affect employee performance are extroversion, agreeableness, conscientiousness, emotional stability, and openness to experience.

Extroversion

Extroversion refers to an individual's tendency to focus on what is external to them. Extroverts are talkative, assertive, and outgoing. Extroverts enjoy spending time or working with other people and tend to get bored when they spend time alone. For example, someone giving a presentation to a group of potential investors needs quite a high degree of extroversion to captivate and convince the investors.

Agreeableness

Agreeableness describes an individual's tendency toward agreement and conformity. It also determines how well-liked someone is. A call center agent who handles customer complaints, for example, could benefit from a high degree of agreeableness. This could help prevent customers from becoming confrontational.

Conscientiousness

Conscientiousness describes an individual's reliability and attention to duty. It's important, for example, that a nurse is conscientious in performing duties that could affect patient health.

Emotional stability

Emotional stability refers to an individual's ability to manage emotional responses, including responses to stress. For example, a person whose job involves counseling others or dealing with crisis situations requires a high degree of emotional stability.

Openness to experience

Individuals' openness to experience determines how ready they are to learn from what's around them. It's associated with curiosity and mental flexibility. A person in a role that requires creative thinking is likely to require a high degree of openness to experience.

Everyone has the main five personality traits, but in varying degrees. For example, one employee might be highly extroverted and another may rank low in this area.

The more extroverted someone is, the more sociable, assertive, and gregarious this person will tend to be.

Extroverts tend to perform better at tasks that require divided attention and short-term memory retrieval. High extroversion coupled with high emotional stability typically results in a "happy personality."

The higher the level of agreeableness someone has, the better this person will be at building good interpersonal relationships. This is because being agreeable makes you more cooperative, warm, and trusting toward others.

Agreeableness coupled with a high level of conscientiousness tends to result in someone who works especially well in teams, or in roles requiring a combination of discipline and cooperation.

Someone who's highly conscientiousness is also responsible, dutiful, and organized, and has good self-control.

Conscientious employees are likely to set ambitious goals for themselves and to work hard to achieve them. In fact, conscientiousness rates as the highest predictor of job performance in virtually any occupation.

Three employees – Arlene, Cody, and Todd – each have varied dominant personality traits, which affect their suitability for particular jobs.

Arlene

Arlene demonstrates a high level of agreeableness. As a result, she has been placed in the Customer Services Department at her company. She's able to deal with customers who have complaints without ever antagonizing them or escalating their frustration. Arlene listens to each customer carefully and addresses any concerns in a polite manner.

Cody

Cody shows a high level of conscientiousness. He's an office administrator and likes to keep everything in his office tidy, and in order. He's generally well organized and is always ready, available, and dependable when his company needs him.

Todd

Todd is highly extroverted. He loves socializing and people generally respond positively to him because of his warm personality. He genuinely enjoys talking to and meeting customers, and shows confidence in himself and his company. This makes him an ideal sales representative.

Someone with a high level of emotional stability is good at dealing with stress and is able to remain calm, self-confident, and secure. An employee in this category is well equipped to handle work pressures and potentially difficult tasks.

However, individuals with high emotional stability may be less alert to potential risks or environmental threats than others. For example, they might give a third-party service provider remote access to a server, or not take into account shifts in customer tastes.

An employee with a high level of openness to experience tends to be creative, curious, and artistically sensitive.

This type of employee also tends to want to acquire more knowledge and adapts easily to change.

Question

Mary is an art director. She loves to read up on different subjects and talk with different people to hear how their views compare to her own strong opinions. She hardly ever loses her temper or gets nervous around the studio. Her office is generally quite cluttered and messy, and she's sometimes late for meetings.

Which personality traits is Mary displaying?

Options:

1. High emotional stability

2. High conscientiousness
3. High agreeableness
4. High openness to experience

Answer

Option 1: This option is correct. Mary demonstrates high emotional stability by remaining calm and in control.

Option 2: This is an incorrect option. Someone highly conscientious wouldn't be late for meetings and would not have a messy, cluttered office.

Option 3: This option is incorrect. Although Mary does like to talk to people, her strong opinions indicate she probably doesn't rate high on the agreeable scale.

Option 4: This option is correct. The fact that Mary likes to read up on different subjects and talk to different people suggests she's highly open to experience. This makes her suited to her creative position as an art director.

Every employee's personality includes a unique combination of the five main personality traits. The key is to identify these traits and their levels, and use them as predictors of employees' overall performance in specific positions.

Todd is highly extroverted. He loves socializing and people generally respond positively to him because of his warm personality. He genuinely enjoys talking to and meeting customers, and shows confidence in himself and his company. This makes him an ideal sales representative.

Question

Match each description of a personality trait to what it predicts about an employee's performance.

Options:

A. High level of extroversion
B. Low level of agreeableness
C. Low level of conscientiousness
D. High level of emotional stability
E. High level of openness to experience

Targets:

1. Performs well in social environments and dealing with people
2. Performs well in competitive environments where the focus is more on the job at hand than

collaborating with people
3. Performs well in relaxed and low-pressure environments
4. Performs well in high-pressure environments
5. Performs well in unpredictable environments

Answer

Someone who is highly extroverted is open and comfortable with relationships. So this person's personality is well suited for this kind of environment.

Someone with low agreeableness enjoys competition and places a high priority on the job. So this person's personality is well suited for this kind of environment.

Someone with low conscientiousness is more laid back and less goal-oriented. This type of person will probably perform best in a relaxed, low-pressure environment.

Someone with high emotional stability remains calm and productive in situations that involve stress. So this type of person is likely to perform well under pressure.

Someone with a high openness to experience enjoys learning and adapting to change. So this type of employee is likely to do well in unpredictable environments.

Section 3 - Individual Perceptions at Work

Section 3 - Individual Perceptions at Work

Your perception can have a direct impact on your organizational behavior. Your perception is affected by factors such as your knowledge, unfulfilled needs and desires, personal interests, and expectations.

You can improve the accuracy of your perceptions by taking any external causes of a person's behavior into account, identifying your own stereotypes and confronting them, evaluating employees based only on objective criteria, and avoiding rash judgments.

What affects perceptions

Suppose one of your colleagues asks for your assistance and you go over to help her. Your manager walks in and shouts at you for wasting time when you know there's a tight deadline to meet. Your manager obviously perceived the situation incorrectly – because you weren't wasting time, but instead only trying to help.

Your perceptions are your interpretations of what you encounter through your senses. People all have slightly different perceptions. For example, many people may view the same incident in an office, but all may form different understandings of what the incident meant.

Your perception of a situation can have a direct impact on your behavior. It can determine whether you perceive a situation correctly, and whether you respond in a way that's appropriate and professional.

Faulty perceptions can also result in bad human resources management, because you may hire the wrong candidates or assign employees to jobs that don't optimize their strengths.

Four main factors contribute to an individual's perceptions:

- the person's existing knowledge,
- unfulfilled needs and desires,
- personal interests, and
- preconceived bias and expectations.

Your existing knowledge can have an effect on the way you perceive things. Over time, you accumulate a base of knowledge through experience, education, and intuition.

Experience

One of the ways you build knowledge is through experience. You acquire knowledge and skills in the course of completing your work and through general life experiences. You may also learn through the experiences of work colleagues, and of family and friends.

Whenever you interpret a new situation, you reflect on your past experience − often without even realizing it − to help you make sense of what you've encountered. Your previous experience may then influence your perception. For example, you're likely to have a negative reaction to an event if similar events in the past had negative outcomes for you. You may also falsely assume you can predict what will happen next based on previous outcomes, when in fact you're facing a completely new situation.

Education

Through formal education, people acquire knowledge in the form of facts and particular skills. They may also be taught practical approaches to handling given situations.

When you encounter new situations, you draw on what you've been taught to make sense of them. If you were taught to interpret a situation in a particular way, it's likely you'll interpret similar, future situations in that way too.

Intuition

Intuition refers to "gut feelings," or the sense that something will turn out in a particular way. Your intuition derives from your past experiences and the ways you interpret the subtleties of situations, even if these are largely subconscious. For example, your intuition may make you feel that one job candidate is being more honest with you than another – even if you can't define exactly what's giving you this impression.

Intuition can affect your perceptions. For example, you may tend to overlook anything that's not in line with what your intuition has caused you to expect.

Your unfulfilled needs and desires can have an effect on your perceptions. So if you're offered something that will meet a specific need, you're more likely to have a positive perception of that offer. The more you perceive something as a positive challenge, the higher you rate it. Your needs and desires can therefore lead you to interpret all kinds of situations based on how they either help or prevent your needs from being met.

Casey works as an arts columnist at a local newspaper. One of his career aspirations is to branch out into current news and events.

When the regular news reporter calls in sick on the day of a major oil refinery accident, the news editor asks

Casey if he would like to cover for the reporter. Casey still needs to finalize his weekly film review column, but he believes he can meet his deadline and report on the accident for the late edition.

Casey perceives the offer as the career opportunity he longs for. But how would Casey have felt about the offer if he hadn't been interested in current news and events coverage? He would probably have perceived the offer as an attempt to jeopardize his own column.

Question

Angela has been an account manager for three years. She's aiming to achieve a promotion to account director. Angela's been overlooked several times in the past for promotions, which have gone to people who put in more overtime than her. When her manager offers her a couple of overtime projects, she jumps at the offer, perceiving it as a great opportunity to prove herself.

Which factors have influenced Angela's perceptions of the situation?

Options:

1. Existing knowledge
2. Unfulfilled needs and desires
3. Personal interests
4. Preconceived biases or expectations

Answer

Option 1: This option is correct. Angela's knowledge affects the way she perceives her manager's offer. One way knowledge is built is through work and life experience. Angela knows from experience that it helps to do extra work if you want to be considered for promotion.

Option 2: This is a correct option. Angela's unfulfilled desire has an effect on the way she perceives her manager's offer. Because she's hoping for a promotion, she views the prospect of doing extra work as an opportunity.

Option 3: This is an incorrect option. Angela's personal interests did not affect her perception of the situation. Angela did not choose to take on the overtime projects because they were of interest to her. Instead, she perceived her manager's offer as a valuable opportunity because of knowledge gained through past experience and because of her unfulfilled desire for a promotion.

Option 4: This is an incorrect option. Angela's preconceived biases or expectations do not have an effect on the way she perceives her manager's offer. Angela's knowledge and her unfulfilled desire affect her perception of her manager's offer.

Another factor that can influence your perception is your individual interests. You may take an interest in something particular that not many other people at your work share. You may be taking external courses in a completely different field from your work or you may have interests in particular areas like politics or current affairs, which can affect your perceptions.

External courses

You may be studying an external course on a subject that isn't associated with your current job, either because you enjoy the subject, or because you want to eventually work in that particular field. In having this interest, it can have an effect on the way you perceive things.

Take Jackie for example. She works in an HR Department and is doing an external course in accounting, as she really wants to learn about the financial aspects of human resource planning. Jackie perceives every HR project proposal with a view of how useful it will be, and whether it's financially viable and will have a good return.

Particular areas

You may have a particular interest in certain areas outside your work. If you develop this interest, the in-depth knowledge you develop can affect the way you perceive things. For example, if you follow market shares in your spare time, you may notice an opportunity for your company to enter a particular market, which you can then reflect in your organizational strategies.

Donald is the director of Sales for a furniture manufacturing company. He's very interested in politics and follows it in his spare time. When a new sales of goods bill is passed into law, Donald's company needs to determine a new strategy that doesn't conflict with this new legislation. Donald may perceive this challenge as more interesting than other colleagues who don't have a personal interest in politics.

The preconceived bias and expectations you hold can affect the way you perceive things. You stereotype certain people because you expect them to perform in a specific way.

For example, you may think a part-time employee who is also a student will work less hard than someone who isn't a student, based on a preconceived notion that students tend to focus on parties and don't work hard. A bias like this can distort your perception. An employee who is also a student may work very hard and be both innovative and enthusiastic.

Question

Sam works as a campaign manager in a social media company. He takes a particular interest in the banking industry. His manager assigns a campaign for an international banking company to Sam's colleague, Tanya, who is nearing retirement age.

Sam believes that because Tanya's so much older than he is, she won't be able to do the project as well as he could. He perceives the situation as unfair.

Which factors have influenced Sam's perceptions of the situation?

Options:

1. Individual interests
2. Expectations
3. Knowledge
4. Unfulfilled need

Answer

Option 1: This is a correct option. It's because Sam takes a particular interest in the banking industry that he hopes to be assigned the bank campaign. In turn, this makes him feel that it's unfair of his manager not to assign the project to him.

Option 2: This is a correct option. Sam has a preconceived expectation, or stereotype, that older employees can't perform as well as he can. This is his basis for thinking that he could do a better job than Tanya.

Option 3: This option is incorrect. In this scenario, it's not specific knowledge that has caused Sam to perceive the work assignment as unfair.

Option 4: This option is incorrect. Sam's perception of the situation isn't specifically affected by an unfulfilled need or desire in this case. It is his interest in the banking industry and the expectation that he can do a job better than someone nearing retirement age.

Improving perceptions

Because your perceptions can have a direct impact on your behavior, it's important to ensure they're as accurate as possible. You can improve your perception by making sure you consider any external causes of others' behavior, identify and confront your stereotypes, evaluate people based only on objective factors, and avoid rash judgments.

Consider external causes

Before you form any perceptions about a person or a situation, it's important to account for any relevant external factors. For instance, circumstances outside an employee's control may affect an employee's behavior.

Consider this example. Marsha has noticed a sudden drop in Jake's productivity. Her first reaction is irritation. However, before talking with Jake, she discovers that Jake has been assigned to help train a new employee. This extra task explains his drop in productivity and Marsha saves herself from sanctioning Jake inappropriately.

Confront stereotypes

You can improve your perceptions of people by identifying and confronting your own stereotypes. This involves recognizing and admitting to particular biases you have, and mentally taking steps to overcome them. You should focus instead purely on facts about a person.

Gwen is trying to hire a new marketing strategist for the social media company she works for. Bill has worked in the marketing field since he graduated from college over 30 years ago. While preparing for her interview with him, she notes that even though he has lots of experience, she tends to perceive older people as not being up-to-date on trends and technologies – a vital qualification in the social media field. Once she's aware she holds this stereotype, she ensures her perception of older candidates doesn't affect her judgment of whether Bill is suitable for the position or not.

Evaluate based on objective factors

A good way of improving your perception is to ensure you make evaluations based only on objective factors. This involves keeping more subjective judgments from affecting the ways you interpret people or situations.

Irene is evaluating several proposals from different people. If she's to be objective, she needs to evaluate each proposal using the same set of criteria – without considering who submitted a proposal or how she feels about his person.

Avoid rash judgments

Everyone jumps to conclusions at some point. To improve your perception, it's helpful to make a conscious effort not to make rash judgments. For example, avoid judging people based on the first impressions they make. Rather get to know someone better before making a judgment.

During a job interview, Justin's initial impression of Dawn is that she lacks confidence and doesn't have the drive needed to succeed in the advertised position. He thinks that this might be a rash judgment and makes a conscious effort to find out more about her. As the interview continues, Dawn relaxes and grows in confidence. Justin realizes that she was just nervous at the beginning of the interview and does in fact have the drive that he's looking for.

Question

Simone is a recent graduate who has been working with a company for a month. Her manager, Melvin, has noted that Simone's productivity is well below average. His first instinct is to be irritated with Simone's poor performance.

What can Melvin do to help ensure he has an accurate perception of the situation?

Options:

1. Take into account that the reason Simone's productivity rate may be down is because she has been attending training

2. Identify his stereotype of graduates and choose not to let it affect his perception

3. Evaluate Simone on the quality of the work she has been doing and ignore the fact that he's skeptical about her

4. Choose to set aside his initial impression and learn more about Simone and her work 5. Evaluate Simone in relation to other employees

6. Find out more about Simone's personal life

Answer

Option 1: This option is correct. You can help to make sure you get the correct perception by always considering external causes. An external cause of Simone's productivity rate being low is that she has been attending training sessions. If Melvin hadn't realized this external cause, he would have had the wrong perception of Simone.

Option 2: This is a correct option. It's useful to identify the stereotypes that you have and confront them. If Melvin realizes that he has a stereotype about recent graduates, he can choose not to let this affect his perception of Simone.

Option 3: This option is correct. You can make your perception better by ensuring you use only objective factors to evaluate people or situations. Melvin can choose to make his evaluation of Simone based on the quality and volume of work she has done, and to ignore his own skepticism about her.

Option 4: This is a correct option. It's important to avoid making rash judgments. Melvin should set aside his first impression of Simone and get to know her better before making a judgment about her behavior.

Option 5: This option is incorrect. Melvin should evaluate Simone using objective criteria. He should also take external factors into account. He shouldn't compare Simone to existing employees because Simone is still new to the company.

Option 6: This is an incorrect option. It's unprofessional to delve into an employee's personal life. Instead Melvin should evaluate Simone objectively, taking external factors that have affected her performance into account as far as possible and avoiding stereotypes.

Section 4 - Factors Affecting Individual Attitudes

Section 4 - Factors Affecting Individual Attitudes

Employees' attitudes can affect their performance and productivity, with corresponding effects on an organization's overall success. Job satisfaction is an example of an attitude. Factors that contribute to employees' job satisfaction include their pay, whether their work is challenging and provides career opportunities, the style adopted by supervisors, their colleagues, and their perceived job status. To help determine employees' levels of job satisfaction, you can check attendance records, check whether employees regularly meet their deadlines, and pay attention to employees' comments and opinions.

Managers can attempt to improve employees' attitudes toward their work by providing constructive feedback, accentuate positive conditions, providing consequences, and serving as positive role models.

What affects attitude

Suppose you've been told to choose a colleague to work on a project with you. You have one colleague who's always enthusiastic and supportive of others, giving constructive criticism in an encouraging way. You have another colleague who's always saying how much he hates his job and who tends to be highly critical of others. Which colleague would you choose to work with? An employee's attitude can have a significant impact on performance and productivity at work.

Your attitude is the way you feel – or your opinions – about a task, a situation, an idea, or a person. You focus an attitude toward something. For example, you can have a positive attitude toward a specific work task. An attitude includes cognitive, affective, and behavioral components.

Cognitive

The cognitive component of an attitude is the part of the attitude that involves conscious thought.

Suppose an employee has a negative attitude toward a certain task. The cognitive part of this attitude could be that the employee thinks the task is pointless and wastes time.

Affective

The affective component of an attitude is the emotion, or feeling, associated with it.

If an employee has a negative attitude toward a certain task, for example, the affective component is the unpleasant or uncomfortable feeling that the employee associates with the task.

Behavioral

The behavioral component of an attitude is the way a person chooses to act as a result of the attitude.

For example, an employee who has a negative attitude toward a certain task may procrastinate, focusing on other work instead of getting the task done.

You can determine whether employees have generally positive or negative attitudes to their work based on certain behaviors, including whether the employees respect their colleagues and their physical environment.

An employee with a positive attitude will show respect for colleagues by providing positive and constructive feedback, and being willing to help when needed. Positive employees also generally respect their physical environment, keeping belongings and ongoing work organized, and looking after office property.

An employee with a negative attitude is more likely to be critical of colleagues' work or even to avoid contact with colleagues. This type of employee is also more likely to act carelessly with office property.

Employee job satisfaction is an example of an attitude. It describes how content employees are with their work and what they get out of it. Proven links exist between job satisfaction and employee behavior, including productivity, absenteeism, and turnover. Factors that affect employees' job satisfaction include their pay, type of work, career opportunities, supervisor style, colleagues, and status.

Salary, or pay, has a direct impact on employees' job satisfaction. Employees who feel they're being paid well generally feel like they're working toward something and are more likely to put in the hard work they're being paid to do.

Employees who think they're not being paid enough are likely to feel unappreciated. This can lead to lower productivity and lower quality of work.

The type of work you do, or the nature of specific tasks, can have an impact on your job satisfaction. For example, factors that affect job satisfaction include whether your work captures your interest, presents challenges, provides you with career opportunities, and involves responsibility.

Captures interest

Employees who find their work interesting are likely to work faster and produce work of higher quality than those who aren't interested in the work they do.

Presents challenges

It's important for a job to present some challenges if it's to retain an employee's attention and interest. This also helps keep an employee alert and constantly learning.

Challenges shouldn't be overwhelming, however, or they can make an employee feel powerless and incapable.

Provides opportunities

Employees who feel their jobs give them career opportunities, or something they can achieve, have higher levels of job satisfaction. Without opportunities to develop, employees are likely to become less productive and engaged.

Involves responsibility

If employees feel like the work they're doing requires responsibility and contributes to an organization's success, they're more likely to feel valued and important. This results in better job satisfaction and better overall performance.

It's important for employees to feel they can develop a career from the work they're doing. Work that has career opportunities will encourage employees to work hard toward organizational and personal goals.

Career opportunities could include promotions, expanding on or learning new skills, or taking on greater responsibilities with added pay benefits.

Question

Cathy has been an administration manager at her company for two years. One of her tasks is to e-mail progress updates to company directors. She often makes sloppy mistakes in the e-mails. When Cathy's manager politely asks her to do something, she rarely does it in a timely fashion. Her desk is extremely messy and she often plays computer games during work hours. Cathy displays a negative attitude.

What factors could have contributed to her attitude?

Options:

1. Cathy feels she's not being paid enough
2. Cathy's type of work doesn't interest her or present challenges
3. Cathy's work doesn't present any career opportunities
4. Cathy feels she isn't capable of doing her job
5. Cathy finds her colleagues unfriendly

Answer

Option 1: This option is correct. Pay can have a dramatic impact on job satisfaction. Cathy may feel she isn't being paid enough and so isn't highly valued. This could contribute to her negative attitude.

Option 2: This is a correct option. The type of work you do can affect your job satisfaction. It's likely that Cathy's work doesn't interest her or present challenges. Instead, it bores her and she'd rather play computer games.

Option 3: This option is correct. Without something clear to work toward, employees may lose motivation. So if Cathy's job doesn't provide her with career opportunities, this could be contributing to her negative attitude.

Option 4: This is an incorrect option. Cathy's job doesn't seem to present her with any challenges, so the reason she's negative about her work isn't that she feels incapable of doing it properly.

Option 5: This option is incorrect. There's no indication in this case that Cathy's colleagues are unfriendly or unfair – and her supervisor is polite when asking her to complete tasks.

Another factor that can affect job satisfaction is the supervisor, or management, style in your workplace. This can include the approach your immediate supervisor, senior managers, or your direct employer take. The more your supervisors show interest in you and your work, the more likely you'll be encouraged to perform well. If a supervisor is concerned with helping you succeed and achieve your goals, you'll also have better job satisfaction.

Your colleagues also have an impact on your job satisfaction. They may contribute to your enjoyment of your work or make your workplace a miserable environment for you to be in.

If your colleagues are unhelpful, unfriendly, and generally make it difficult for you to get your work done, you're likely to have lower job satisfaction. It can be equally demoralizing if the people you're working with don't perform well.

Gilbert works in a team of marketing strategists that arranges group projects for big clients. Gilbert finds that he's always left to draw up the final reports and record discussions on his own.

His colleagues are also rude to him and don't take his ideas into account. Because they've been with the company longer than him, he feels he can't approach them about this.

Gilbert has low job satisfaction as a direct result of his colleagues' behavior.

The status of your job can have an effect on your job satisfaction. If employees are happy with their job status, they're likely to be proud of their work and willing to work hard to maintain their status. Employees who aren't happy with their status may simply not care and produce work of lower quality.

Question

Jason's supervisor asks him very politely if he would put in a few extra hours to assist with training a new employee. The supervisor says she believes Jason will do a great job. Another of Jason's colleagues overhears this and offers to help. Jason believes that he's part of a strong team and that any new employee can be successfully trained as a strong team player. Jason tells his supervisor that he's happy to help and seems enthusiastic. Jason is displaying a positive attitude.

What factors could have contributed to this?

Options:

1. Jason believes that his supervisor cares about all the employees' success

2. Jason's colleagues are friendly and willing to help

3. Jason's team members are proud of their status and believe the new employee is able to achieve the same

4. Jason doesn't take an interest in his work

5. Jason feels like he's not being paid enough

Answer

Option 1: This option is correct. Jason's supervisor appears to care about his development and success. This is likely to contribute to Jason's positive attitude.

Option 2: This is a correct option. One of Jason's colleagues offers to help Jason. Friendly and supportive colleagues can help improve everyone's job satisfaction.

Option 3: This option is correct. The status of your job can affect your attitude toward it. Jason is proud of his status and wants to help the new employee achieve the same satisfaction.

Option 4: This is an incorrect option. Jason displays a positive attitude and seems proud of the strong team that he's a part of. If he didn't find his work interesting, it's unlikely he'd feel this way.

Option 5: This option is incorrect. If Jason believed he wasn't being paid enough, he'd probably have a more negative attitude toward his work.

Ways to help establish employees' job satisfaction include examining their attendance records and punctuality, observing whether they meet deadlines and demonstrate good time management, and paying attention to their comments and opinions.

Typically employees with low job satisfaction are absent or late more often than employees who enjoy their jobs. So attendance records can help you identify employees with particular morale problems.

Similarly, employees with low job satisfaction are less likely than others to meet deadlines consistently and to manage their time well. They may simply lack the motivation to do this.

A final way to assess employees' job satisfaction is to listen to their comments and opinions at work. For example, if an employee often makes derogatory comments such as "I don't care," it probably indicates low job satisfaction.

Improving attitudes

Managers can reduce turnover and boost performance when they try to improve employees' attitudes to their work. They can do this by providing employees with appropriate feedback, highlighting positive conditions, providing consequences, and being positive role models.

Providing feedback

Managers can help employees become aware of negative attitudes. They should also explain how these attitudes affect their colleagues' work. It's important to deliver this type of feedback in a constructive and supportive manner. If a manager delivers feedback in a threatening or intimidating way, it may make an employee's already-poor attitude even more negative.

Highlighting positive conditions

A manager can highlight the positive conditions that are provided for the employees to encourage them to help improve their attitudes. For example, a manager could highlight the fact that employees are provided with a constant support system where they can ask for help at any time.

Providing consequences

Managers can present rewards and opportunities as encouragement for employees to maintain the existing positive attitudes and keep any negative attitudes from spreading. For example, a manager could provide monetary bonuses for good performance to make employees feel appreciated and rewarded for their hard work.

Being positive role models

A manager should be a positive role model for employees, conveying a positive attitude at all times. For example, a manager's enthusiasm about a project may affect employees positively, overcoming their initially negative attitudes toward the work.

Question

Jake, a manager, notices that one of his employees, Maria, has a negative attitude toward a new project. Maria is arriving at the office later and later, and her negative comments are causing other employees to begin thinking negatively too.

What can Jake do to improve Maria's attitude?

Options:

1. Jake can call Maria in for a meeting to describe to her the negative affects that are coming from her attitude

2. Jake can draw Maria's attention to what she can achieve with the project

3. Jake can offer monetary incentives to all the employees including Maria

4. Jake can show Maria that he's positive about the project and the team's ability to complete it

5. Jake can threaten to fire Maria in front of other employees

6. Jake can tell Maria that she can do another project instead

Answer

Option 1: This is a correct option. A manager may improve an employee's attitude simply by providing constructive feedback, and identifying the attitude and the undesirable effects it has on the employee's work and colleagues.

Option 2: This option is correct. A manager can help improve an employee's attitude by emphasizing the positive. By pointing out what Maria can achieve through the project, Jake encourages her to be more positive about it.

Option 3: This is a correct option. A manager can present encouragement in the way of rewards and benefits to help improve employees' attitudes. By providing a monetary incentive, Jake may encourage Maria to think more positively about the project.

Option 4: This option is correct. Employees often respect their managers and may model their attitudes. If Jake shows that he's positive and enthusiastic about the project, it may encourage Maria to adopt the same attitude.

Option 5: This is an incorrect option. Managers shouldn't give feedback in a threatening way. Doing this can make an employee's attitude even more negative. Instead, Jake should call Maria in for a meeting and explain the effects that her negative attitude is having in a way that's supportive.

Option 6: This option is incorrect. Allowing Maria to do something else instead may be unfair to other employees. It would be better for Jake to try to improve Maria's attitude about the relevant project.

CHAPTER 2 - Groups

CHAPTER 2 - Groups

Section 1 - Groups in Organizations

Section 1 - Groups in Organizations

A group consists of two or more people who work toward achieving a common goal and who have a shared identity. External factors that can affect the performance of a group include regulations, the hierarchy of power, evaluation systems, reward programs, and organizational culture. Other factors include leadership, organization size, and the personal characteristics of group members.

Groups benefit an organization in several ways. Skills and knowledge can be pooled, employees feel more secure in groups – resulting in greater creativity, and group members are more motivated.

An effective group is one in which members have the necessary technical and interpersonal skills, agree on rules of conduct, set measurable goals, have a shared purpose, are interdependent, and feel free to express themselves.

Groups in an organization

Can you imagine running a business without organizing employees into groups of any type? Anyone who's attempted this would not have recognized the benefits that properly managed groups have to offer. Groups provide cohesion between employees, which makes it easy to steer different individuals' efforts in a common direction.

In the context of an organization, a group is two or more people who share a common identity, adhere to norms they hold in common, and work together to achieve a shared goal. The people in a group are typically accountable to a supervisor or manager.

The interaction between members defines the group and determines who's part of it. However, members don't necessarily interact face-to-face. For example, telecommuting workers may form a group although they work off-site – and they may communicate largely by e-mail rather than verbally.

All members of a group share a common goal or purpose. Examples could range from capturing a new segment of the market to simply fixing the office water cooler.

Groups have a significant effect on the behavior of individuals within an organization for two main reasons:

- group members can acquire shared beliefs, attitudes, values, and behaviors, and
- group members can be a positive influence on one another and so increase productivity.

Groups are a natural social phenomenon. In an organization, they can be either formal or informal.

Formal

Formal groups are established intentionally to achieve goals of an organizational nature. They're managed and they focus on the completion of set tasks.

Informal

Informal groups are established casually, outside the direction of the organization. They're social in nature and their members focus on common interests, rather than on completing particular tasks. Depending on their norms, they can help or damage an organization.

For organizations, well-managed groups can have several important advantages:

- they can perform complex interdependent tasks beyond the scope of individuals,
- they can find creative new solutions to problems by drawing on the insights and ideas of multiple individuals,
- they can coordinate interdepartmental efforts,

- they can perform problem solving at different levels with different inputs,
- they can implement complex decisions, and
- they can train and socialize newcomers.

Groups can also have benefits for the individuals who belong to them. Group membership can make an individual feel affiliated, affirm the individual's self-esteem and sense of belonging, and help the individual perceive a social reality. It can also reduce an individual's anxiety or insecurity, and help solve interpersonal problems.

Various factors affect group performance. It's important for a manager to understand these and, where possible, to use them to optimize a group's potential. Among the external factors that can affect group performance are regulations, the hierarchy of power that affects the group, evaluation systems, reward programs, and organizational culture.

Regulations

Regulations are the standards and rules that an organization and its employees must follow. Groups within an organization are equally subject to these regulations, which determine acceptable types of behavior.

Hierarchy of power

The hierarchy of power in an organization refers to its official leadership structure – for example with teams led by managers, who in turn report to more senior managers. It can affect the ways a group is permitted to make and act on decisions.

Evaluation systems

Systems for evaluating performance may encourage high levels of productivity and efficiency. They can be designed to focus on group performance, as well as on individual performance.

Reward programs

Reward programs are used to reward positive behavior and motivate employees to exhibit such behaviors in the future. They may reward members of a group for their collective performance, rather than only rewarding employees for their individual efforts.

Organizational culture

Organizational culture refers to the physical and emotional environment in an organization. Physical culture includes cleanliness, noise levels, and lighting. Emotional culture includes group norms and beliefs, as well as the support and degree of empowerment given to employees.

Of the intrinsic features that affect group performance, leadership is one of the most important. Whether they're officially appointed or emerge more informally, effective leaders play an important role in determining the productivity and attitudes within any group.

Leaders promote high group productivity when they show a positive attitude, commitment to their jobs, and respect for their organization. Others admire them because they set a good example.

Group size is another important factor. Generally, a smaller group is better suited to action-oriented tasks. Its members can connect more quickly than members of large groups.

A larger group is useful for tasks requiring abstract or creative thinking because it lets you draw on more people's insights.

A final factor that affects group performance is the personal characteristics of group members. Generally, a group is more cohesive and easier to manage if team members have similar characteristics, such as similarities in age, gender, marital status, education, and experience.

However, a group with members who are too similar is likely to be less creative than a group with more diverse membership.

Question

Which statements are true of groups in organizations?

Options:

1. A group stifles individual creativity and encourages strife

2. Members of a group share a common purpose

3. The personalities of group members will affect their capacity to work well together

4. To form a group, individuals have to communicate face-to-face on a regular basis

5. A group will probably be less effective if it has to work in a very noisy environment

Answer

Option 1: This is an incorrect option. Belonging to a group can make an individual feel more secure, and this can actually foster creativity. Groups only encourage strife and stifle creativity if they're badly managed.

Option 2: This option is correct. A group in the organizational sense consists of people united by a common goal.

Option 3: This is a correct option. Personal characteristics affect the way people in a group work together.

Option 4: This is an incorrect option. A group can include off-site members, and these members may communicate in different ways – for example via e-mail.

Option 5: This is a correct option. Physical factors such as cleanliness, noise levels, and lighting can all affect a group's performance.

Benefits of understanding groups

Managers who understand groups and the factors that affect their performance can make their groups much more effective in a variety of ways. They can ensure members capitalize on the benefits of working in groups.

Question

A group of designers is developing concepts for a new product launch. The group members have successfully worked on similar projects before and are all keen to apply their talents.

What do you think are the benefits of them working as a group?

Options:

1. They can let others take the responsibility if something goes wrong
2. They can brainstorm and be more creative together
3. They can find security in working as one unit

4. They can get the job done faster as a group
5. They can eliminate all risk from what they're doing
Answer

Actually, working as a group will enable the designers to brainstorm and is likely to make them feel more secure and finish the job faster.

An effective group offers many benefits:

- group members can share technical skills and knowledge,
- group members feel bolder and more secure,
- group members motivate and inspire greater creativity in each other,
- group members are more ready to commit to action, and
- group members make better decisions.

As a group, members can combine their knowledge, talents, and skills in a highly productive collaboration. Working together is a motivating experience with many opportunities for positive interaction.

In a group context, members typically feel more secure and less daunted by projects and more ready to tackle a project than individuals would. This is because of the collective knowledge and skills they share, and because of the support they offer one another.

Groups are generally more willing to take creative risks than individuals. In a group setting, fear doesn't stifle the creative impulse as much because they share a common purpose.

In an organization, group members are more willing to commit to action because they assume individual responsibility for their work and know they are answerable to the group.

Group members make better decisions within an organization because they integrate different viewpoints before taking action.

Characteristics of effective groups
Question

A group of engineers decides to add a second phase to a project it's currently working on. Each group member takes responsibility for one aspect of the project. If a group member disagrees about something, the others will listen to that person's objections because members of this group respect each other's skills and expertise.

How effective do you think this group is?

Options:

1. Very effective
2. Reasonably effective
3. Not effective

Answer

Option 1: Yes, this group is very effective because members can form agreement, cooperate, and work in a culture of respect.

Option 2: In fact, this group is very effective because its members reach agreement, cooperate, and respect each other.

Option 3: Actually, this group is very effective because its members can find agreement, cooperate, and respect each other.

As you can deduce from considering their merits, effective groups in an organization have six main characteristics:

- the members agree on rules of conduct,
- the group has measurable goals,
- the group has a sense of common purpose,
- together, members have the required range of technical and interpersonal skills,
- there are member interdependencies, with all members depending in some way on others, and
- members feel free to express themselves.

Rules of conduct are regulations governing professional behavior. When group members develop and adhere to these rules, it shows that they consider themselves accountable to one another. They agree to behave in specific ways for the good of the group, and to take responsibility for their actions. This can result in work of a higher quality.

Examples of rules of conduct may be that all group members must be punctual for meetings, meet their deadlines, and always be courteous to clients and other stakeholders.

If a group has measurable goals, both its manager and the group members themselves can track progress according to objective criteria, usually within a given time frame. For example, measurable goals for a group might include reducing budget costs by 12% by the end of the business quarter, increasing market share by 8% by the end of the year, or increasing customer satisfaction by 8 points on a scorecard.

Question

A group of engineers is developing a new product for an important client. The group decides that the second phase of product development must be complete within a month. Group members also agree in writing that all of them will be in the laboratory by 8:00 a.m. every morning to start work. A senior manager supervises the group.

Which are the features that help make this group effective?

Options:

1. There are agreed rules of conduct
2. Each member is accountable to a senior manager
3. The group has a measurable goal
4. The group puts all decisions in writing

Answer

Option 1: This is a correct option. Formally committing to a start time each morning is an example of a group agreeing on rules of conduct, which is one of the indicators of group success.

Option 2: This is an incorrect option. A supervisor wouldn't have to micromanage an effective group. Instead, the group's members feel responsible and accountable to each other.

Option 3: This is a correct option. The group in this example is committed to the specific objective of completing a development phase within a month.

Option 4: This is an incorrect option. Although the group may put its rules of conduct in writing, it is not required for the group to be effective.

A common purpose is the cornerstone of a successful group. This isn't necessarily the same as a shared task. It defines what a group is setting out to achieve, rather than the specific work it will do.

For example, the common purpose of a group in an advertising company could be to win a major client. It could also be to put the company on the map as a champion innovator.

A shared purpose can be a source of inspiration for all members of a group, uniting them and making them feel valued and proud of their work.

In an effective group, the technical and interpersonal skills of individual members are matched to the group's purpose.

For example, members of a successful software development group have the programming expertise

and creative skills to build required systems. They are equally skilled at negotiating the often tricky give- and-take that occurs at an interpersonal level in a group environment.

In an effective group, group members can depend on each other for support and draw on one another's skills. Member interdependencies also create cohesion, which can lead to innovative thinking and greater willingness to take risks.

For example, a group working in a publishing house might include members with sub-editing skills and production skills, expertise in a particular subject, and design skills. The members of the group depend on each other's abilities.

A further characteristic of an effective group is that members feel free to express themselves. They can state their opinions and make suggestions without fear of scorn or ridicule.

Question

An IT company is developing new software for a client. A group of programmers is tasked with implementing a system using a programming language with which they are all familiar. Each programmer works on a module of the system and requests help from colleagues when needed. Between them, the programmers have a wealth of technical knowledge. When one programmer has an idea for taking the system further, she feels free to suggest it. The group is determined to make the new system a success and to set the bar high for other systems of its kind.

Which are the qualities that help make this group effective?

Options:

1. The members depend on one another's skills and expertise

2. The group members work efficiently on their own until called upon to collaborate

3. The group works in a spirit of mutual respect and openness

4. The group has established definite rules of conduct

5. The group members have a shared purpose

Answer

Option 1: This is a correct option. Interdependencies among members of a group make for a more effective group. In this case, all the programmers contribute particular expertise and rely on one another.

Option 2: This is an incorrect option. Although the programmers work on separate modules of the project, communication and collaboration take place regularly.

Option 3: This is a correct option. The scenario suggests that group members feel free to communicate their ideas.

Option 4: This is an incorrect option. The scenario in this example doesn't indicate that the programmers have established particular rules of conduct.

Option 5: This is a correct option. All members of the group in this example are aiming to develop a system to a very high standard. This aspiration unites them.

Question

A group of marketing specialists in an asset management company is responsible for marketing a fund. The group members are aiming to sell 30% of the fund within six months. They work well together and support one another. They've also agreed to adhere to specific guidelines, including how to communicate with prospective buyers. A manager supervises the group's progress and allocates tasks.

Which characteristics help make this group effective?

Options:

1. A leader determines the work output of each group member

2. The group has a measurable goal

3. The group members have the interpersonal skills that enable them to collaborate well

4. Group members have different ideas about what constitutes professional behavior

5. Group members have agreed to specific rules of conduct

Answer

Option 1: This is an incorrect option. Although effective groups often do have leaders, the emphasis is on all members sharing a common sense of purpose and being accountable to one another.

Option 2: This is a correct option. The group's sales target is measurable and can be used to motivate and track progress.

Option 3: This is a correct option. Members work well together and support one another, indicating they have the interpersonal skills needed for effective collaboration.

Option 4: This is an incorrect option. Group members agree on a code of standards that applies to all of them.

Option 5: This is a correct option. The group members have agreed to adhere to specific guidelines. This indicates their willingness to be accountable to one another.

Section 2 - Resistance and Conflicting Priorities in Groups

Section 2 - Resistance and Conflicting Priorities in Groups

Resistance to collaboration can cause groups to fail. This resistance can come from outsiders or individuals within the group.

Various techniques can combat internal resistance, including listening to detractors, encouraging enthusiasts, and strategically promoting desired behaviors. External resistance can be dealt with by publicizing short-term achievements, enlisting sponsor support, and exercising damage limitation.

Groups can also fail when individual members have conflicts of priorities. To resolve these conflicts, you can use joint priority setting, meeting management, cross-training, and recognition of efforts toward group tasks.

Resistance to collaboration

Working in groups can benefit organizations in many ways, but when groups fail, the consequences can be disastrous. Tension, infighting, and lack of cooperation can result in decreased productivity, financial losses, and damaging publicity for the organization.

Symptoms that a group isn't operating effectively include ill-defined goals, lack of commitment, guarded communication, and negative conflict.

Three major challenges to building effective groups are resistance to collaboration, conflict of priorities, and intra-group conflict. Resistance to collaboration can come from both internal and external sources.

Internal

Some group members might feel that their areas of work are so specialized that they should be completely independent.

For others, collaboration means loss of existing autonomy over their tasks. Whereas before they had one supervisor telling them what to do, now they will be subject to the whims of teammates who lack functional knowledge and managerial skills. And whereas before they could confine themselves to tasks they do well, they are now expected to work with less-experienced or less-skilled group members – an added responsibility for which they don't get paid.

External

Resistance may come from outside the group. For example, people whose cooperation you need might snub your group because they're used to dealing only with management. Others may criticize the group if it doesn't produce immediate results.

There may be personal reasons for external resistance. Outside individuals or teams may be worried that your success will make their performance figures look bad.

Finally, management could be the problem if it fails to provide your group with the resources and support it initially promised.

Take Stefan, an enthusiastic editor at a company that publishes a weekly newspaper. Stefan wants to initiate a new monthly magazine for inclusion in the newspaper. Management allows several staff members to join him in forming a project group. However, while working on the first issue, he finds that the group isn't performing as well as he hoped it would.

In Stefan's group, Andrew – a journalist – resents having to mentor Violet, who's an intern. He has always worked well independently, and feels that working with

Violet is slowing him down and preventing him from turning in quality stories.

Joe – a photographer – doesn't like the fact that the company's graphic artist, who has had conflicts with Stefan in the past, seems to be doing little or no work on the photographs Joe has taken for the new magazine.

And Stefan finds that although the newspaper's senior managers initially seemed enthusiastic about the magazine, they aren't giving him enough funding to make the project a success.

Question

Members of Stefan's group are failing to work together successfully because of resistance from various sources.

Match each category of resistance with the examples that illustrate it. A category may match to more than one example.

Options:

A. Internal resistance B. External resistance

Targets:

1. Andrew dislikes having to mentor Violet

2. Joe isn't getting cooperation from the company's graphic artist

3. Senior management isn't providing Stefan with sufficient funds

Answer

One of the typical reasons for internal resistance to collaboration is the feeling that one's work is being interrupted. Andrew resents having to mentor Violet when he could be getting on with his own work.

Joe's frustration at not getting the help he needs from a graphic artist is an example of external resistance. The graphic artist isn't a direct member of Stefan's group.

Stefan's lack of support from senior management is an example of external resistance. The managers initially supported the idea of the magazine, but they aren't giving Stefan sufficient financial backing to make the project work.

Overcoming resistance

There are three good ways of responding to internal resistance to group collaboration: listen to detractors, encourage enthusiasts, and strategically promote desired behaviors.

Listen to detractors

It can get tiring constantly listening to detractors' criticism. But to win them over, you need to listen to their complaints and ask them to suggest solutions. By responding constructively to their concerns, you make detractors feel that their opinions count and so encourage buy-in.

For example, certain group members complain that the physical office layout makes group collaboration difficult. Get them to draw a new floor plan and rearrange the furniture so that collaboration becomes easier.

Encourage enthusiasts

78

If some group members oppose collaboration, you can use the enthusiasm of their more positive colleagues to spread team spirit. Visibly provide extra support to the more enthusiastic group members by hearing their problems, giving them advice, and acting as champion for their causes.

This boosts the confidence of the already-enthusiastic members, which helps them to encourage others to get into the team spirit. It also shows the negative individuals the value of a positive attitude toward group work.

For example, if enthusiastic group members are struggling to adapt to a new reporting system, bring in an expert to help them understand any tricky elements of the system.

Strategically promote behaviors

In promoting collaboration, it helps to be strategic in the way you express desired behaviors. Terms like "teamwork" and "joint responsibility" may evoke negative feelings in the minds of some, due to negative past experiences. They may have no problem with doing what's required, but the terms you use might automatically cause them to resist. So rather focus on what those terms actually mean and on what behaviors you want people to exhibit.

For example, instead of telling a senior group member to "mentor" or "train" a junior member, rather ask the senior person to show the junior person how to do a particular task.

Andrew, one of the journalists in Stefan's group, is resistant to collaboration. He feels that group work just isn't his style and that inexperienced members of the group are wasting his time with trivial queries.

Question

Which actions should Stefan take to break down Andrew's resistance to collaboration?

Options:

1. Call everyone together and explain that the group is failing because Andrew is behaving selfishly and not being a "team player"

2. Ask Andrew to estimate how many minor problems Violet asks him about per day, and to think of some ways to make her more self-empowered

3. Ask Andrew to be patient with Violet, and remind him that the managers would be upset if they heard about his poor attitude toward mentoring

4. Explain to Andrew that he respects his valuable experience, and wants him to share it by showing Violet how to carry out certain journalistic tasks

Answer

Option 1: This is an incorrect option. Publicly criticizing Andrew would anger and embarrass him personally, and could cause tremendous tension within the group.

Option 2: This option is correct. By listening to Andrew's complaints about Violet's requests, Stefan can make Andrew feel valued, and give him a sense of control over the issues bothering him.

Option 3: This option is incorrect. Encouraging patience does little to convince Andrew that Stefan is taking his problem seriously. Additionally, issuing a subtle threat against Andrew only makes things worse.

Option 4: This option is correct. Andrew is uneasy with the "mentor" title, so by strategically focusing on actual behaviors, Stefan can decrease Andrew's resistance.

There are three recommended ways of dealing with external resistance to group collaboration. Publicize the group's short-term achievements, enlist sponsor support to help you increase the group's credibility with outside contacts, and act quickly to limit the damage, if for example, promised deadlines have been missed.

Publicize short-term achievements

Outsiders who oppose your group may undervalue your group's contribution to the organization, and feel that your group's work is a waste of money. To preempt this criticism, you should document and publicize the short-term milestones or achievements your group accomplishes. This gives you proof that your group is productive and is providing value to the company.

For example, your group is systematically rolling out a new, company-wide administration system. As each department settles in to the system, you can publish statistics that show how the system's built-in efficiencies have provided time savings.

Enlist sponsor support

Your group or project sponsor is usually a well-respected, powerful figure within the organization. When other groups, individuals, or even management make things difficult for your group, you can call in the help of this sponsor. The sponsor's influence can go a long way toward solving your problems and building credibility for your group.

For example, if management seems too busy to consider your request for additional funding, ask your sponsor to give a short presentation explaining how important the request is and how it can boost your group's performance.

Act quickly to limit damage

Outsiders may be waiting for your group to fail or miss a deadline, and such failures encourage their negativity. To counter this, you should react quickly to minimize the fallout. Explain how your group plans to redeem itself and publicize the group's successes. It's best always to keep track of your group's progress so that you can anticipate and plan for situations like this.

For example, your group is developing a new software component and misses a deadline. Explain that your new deadline will enable you to produce an even better product.

Corbin, the company's graphic artist, who doesn't want Stefan's group to succeed, is undermining Stefan's initiative. Corbin puts in minimal effort when he's asked to work on material for the magazine, and this lack of effort is slowing down the group's progress.

Corbin often tells group members that the magazine won't succeed and that they should all just quit and go back to their "real" jobs. He notes that a previous, similar initiative failed and believes that he doesn't have to put in much effort for this project, which he thinks is doomed to failure.

Another external obstacle is senior management, who believes that Stefan's project isn't progressing.

As a result, senior management is keeping the group on a low budget.

These restrictions are evident when some of the journalists struggle to do their research and miss a publishing deadline because they don't have access to the online journals they require.

Management refuses to purchase the required journal subscriptions, so the journalists have to go through a lengthy, alternative process to find the information they need.

Question

What can Stefan do to break down the external resistance his group faces?

Options:

1. Offer senior managers a sneak peak at the magazine, and regularly update them as the group achieves each milestone

2. Explain to management that its refusal to purchase the journal subscriptions has delayed the magazine's publishing date

3. Tell Corbin that if he continues to sabotage the group's work, Stefan will ask management to fire him

4. Ask Robert, the project sponsor, to remind Corbin that management expects professional conduct from him – regardless of his personal issues with Stefan

5. Explain to management that the group is using the delayed deadline to enhance the magazine's layout, which will increase its attractiveness to readers

Answer

Option 1: This option is correct. By publicizing the group's short-term achievements and offering a preview, Stefan can show his group's productivity.

Option 2: This is an incorrect option. Although the excuse is valid, blaming management does not help lower the resistance and it may even make things worse.

Option 3: This option is incorrect. Given the history of conflict between Stefan and Corbin, a threat could make Corbin even more defiant and resistant.

Option 4: This is a correct option. By drawing on the support of the group sponsor, Stefan can use Robert's influence to help limit the destructive effects of the personal conflict Corbin has with Stefan.

Option 5: This option is correct. By exercising damage limitation, Stefan can show management that his group makes maximum use of its time, and has taken a missed deadline as an opportunity to improve the magazine's quality.

Correcting conflicts of priority

Conflicting priorities within a group can hamper group performance. Symptoms of conflicting priorities are group members being too busy for group projects or meetings, and group members choosing to shortchange group and administration tasks to prioritize functional tasks.

Several factors could cause individual members to be too busy to contribute properly to a group. They may be working on many different project teams at the same time, or be assigned extra ongoing work that's not associated with any group effort. Or the group may be making poor use of its time.

When group members choose to focus on functional tasks rather than group and administration tasks, an underlying reason could be a lack of motivation. For example, if the organization's rewards system emphasizes functional performance rather than group results, individuals may not have much incentive to give their group work priority.

The problem could also be structural. There may be no processes in place to help employees combine their functional work with group and administrative tasks.

If individual members are too busy with other work to contribute properly to a group, you can use several strategies to resolve their conflicting priorities. These include joint priority setting, meeting management, and finding either temporary or permanent replacements.

Joint priority setting

Individuals meet with their managers to discuss and agree on the order of priority for different tasks and work. This is important because when functional managers are involved in the priority setting, employees have clear guidance as to what they need to focus on and what is less important.

Meeting management

Group leaders manage meetings very carefully to ensure that group members' time is not wasted. Group leaders schedule meetings at convenient times, limit meeting attendance to only the relevant people, and ensure that meeting agendas are tightly adhered to.

Temporary replacement

Temporary replacement is useful when group members are unable to fulfill their group responsibilities for a limited period of time. You ask these individuals to recommend temporary replacements that have the sufficient skills and knowledge to take over their work until they return.

Permanent replacement

Permanent replacement is necessary when group members are either no longer able, or no longer willing, to fulfill their group responsibilities. You ask management to identify replacements that have appropriate skills and knowledge to take over the roles permanently.

Another of Stefan's problems is that the magazine's fact checker, Natasha, seems to be contributing very little to the group's work. Follow along as Stefan discusses the problem with Natasha.

Stefan: I need to speak to you about your work rate on the magazine. It seems you're procrastinating a lot, and you don't even come to the meetings any more.

Stefan is concerned.

Natasha: It's not procrastination...I'm just busy. My other manager, James, is giving me so much work that I can barely keep up with my regular job – let alone the magazine.

Natasha is tired and frustrated.

Natasha: And on top of that, Anna, the head of Marketing is giving me extra work – she's on a new promotional drive.

Natasha is frustrated.

Stefan: Wow. I didn't realize you were under so much pressure. However, you're the best at doing what you do, so I really want to keep you on this project. When do you expect things to calm down with your other work?

Stefan is sympathetic.

Natasha: The promotional stuff, maybe a couple of weeks. And James hasn't given us a definite date, but he thinks things should settle down pretty soon.

Stefan: OK, well I'll have to come up with a solution. Thanks Natasha. I'll get back to you soon.

Question

Natasha's other work is keeping her too busy for her to contribute to the magazine.

Which solutions can Stefan apply to resolve this situation?

Options:

1. Meet with Natasha and her other managers, and agree on her priorities

2. Rearrange the meeting schedule so that Natasha can spend minimal time at group meetings

3. Ask senior management to assign a permanent replacement for Natasha

4. Ask Natasha to suggest a stand-in that can do her job until her other work calms down

5. Do nothing and wait for Natasha's other workload to decrease

Answer

Option 1: This option is correct. By jointly setting Natasha's priorities, Stefan can help Natasha to split her time in a way that satisfies all parties.

Option 2: This is a correct option. By managing meetings around Natasha's time pressure, Stefan can ensure Natasha can still contribute even though her time is limited.

Option 3: This option is incorrect. Natasha's heavy workload is only temporary, so permanent replacement would be unwise – especially since Stefan wants to keep her on the project.

Option 4: This option is correct. A temporary replacement would ensure that Natasha's work gets done immediately, but allow her to return to the group when she's able to.

Option 5: This is an incorrect option. Stefan needs Natasha's work to be done immediately, so leaving things as is does not solve his problem.

When individuals choose functional tasks over group and administration tasks, you can resolve these conflicting priorities by using cross-training, motivation, and recognition.

Cross-training

You can diversify within your group by cross-training members so that they can take over from members who neglect administration or group tasks. This gives you backup inside the group, without the need to recruit replacements.

Motivation

You can motivate individuals by explaining how they can benefit from group tasks. Point out the new skills they can build, which can help them further their career advancement.

Recognition

You can reward individuals for carrying out group tasks by providing nonmonetary recognition. Thank the individual privately or in front of the rest of the group; or get the company CEO to send a personal thank-you to the individual. Or initiate a monthly award for the best-performing group member. As an add-on to this, you could provide a nonmonetary reward such as an afternoon off.

Although Joe – the photographer for Stefan's magazine – is enthusiastic about his photographic work on the magazine, Stefan finds that he neglects the administrative side of his magazine assignments.

He discusses this with Joe, and finds that Joe's other manager hasn't given Joe guidance on how to split his time between the magazine and his regular work.

As a result, Joe considers his administrative duties as unimportant tasks, which he can deal with some other time.

Joe also regularly misses group meetings, saying that he has better things to do than sit in gatherings that won't benefit him financially.

This statement stems from the fact that the magazine is still an experimental venture – Joe won't be paid a bonus for this work yet. He'll only receive a bonus much later, if the magazine becomes profitable.

Question

What can Stefan do to increase Joe's commitment to the magazine?

Options:

1. Ask Joe to train the magazine's journalists in photography, so that they can fill in for Joe when required

2. At the newspaper's next general staff meeting, publicly congratulate Joe on his outstanding contributions to the magazine

3. Remind Joe that his dedicated participation in the magazine could open the door to higher positions in the newspaper

4. Threaten to replace Joe with a new photographer if he keeps skipping meetings

Answer

Option 1: This option is incorrect. The issue isn't Joe's neglect of his photography work. It's Joe's neglect of his administrative tasks.

Option 2: This is a correct option. Giving Joe public recognition boosts his confidence and self-esteem – which can act as a strong motivator.

Option 3: This option is correct. Explaining the career advancement opportunities on offer can motivate Joe to be more committed to the magazine and the group.

Option 4: This is an incorrect option. Threatening Joe isn't a good tactic because it doesn't address the root causes of Joe's lack of commitment – conflicting priorities and lack of motivation.

Section 3 - Conflicts within Groups

Section 3 - Conflicts within Groups

Conflict is inevitable when people work in groups. Some conflict can be good, or functional, but if it's dysfunctional, it can have a negative impact on group performance. Causes of dysfunctional conflict include unresolved prior conflict, role ambiguity, and task interdependencies.

An effective process for resolving conflict includes five steps – assessing the situation, identifying the source of conflict, evaluating the personalities involved, addressing expectations, and determining a course of action.

Causes of group conflict

Whenever people are in close proximity for an extended period, it's inevitable that some conflicts will arise. This applies equally in the workplace. So for organizations, one of the biggest challenges in maintaining effective groups is negotiating conflict. Constant arguments between employees can hamper a group's performance, and affect the members' job performance and satisfaction. For an organization, this can translate into low productivity, higher employee absenteeism and turnover, and lower profits.

Conflict involves disagreement among people due to opposing interests, principles, ideas, wants, or needs. But not all conflict is bad for an organization. There is functional conflict, which is good, and dysfunctional conflict, which is bad.

Functional conflict

Good – or functional – conflict can ensure issues are raised and addressed. It increases information flow between employees and so improves decision-making. It also helps groups find creative ways to improve performance.

For example, if team members disagree with one another about the best way to solve a particular problem, they're more likely to assess all the alternatives and arrive at the best solution.

Dysfunctional conflict

Bad – or dysfunctional – conflict works to the disadvantage of groups and organizations. It diverts energies, damages group cohesion, involves personal hostilities, and creates a negative environment for employees.

For instance, a personal disagreement might make it difficult for two team members to work together at all.

In a group, dysfunctional conflict can take the form of either an emotional conflict or a substantive conflict.

Emotional conflict involves what's commonly known as a "clash of personalities." It occurs when people take issue with one another, and can involve feelings of anger, mistrust, dislike, fear, and resentment. For example, two employees may argue because they dislike or resent one another.

A substantive conflict is a disagreement about how an objective or goal will be pursued, or about what's needed to accomplish it. For example, two employees may argue about the best way to design a product or complete a proposal.

In group contexts, there are three main causes of conflict. These are unresolved prior conflict, role ambiguity, and task interdependency.

Unresolved prior conflict

If conflicts aren't resolved, they often get buried. Then they may resurface in the future as the basis for conflicts over the same or related matters.

As an example, two employees argue over a parking spot and a solution isn't found. The next time they argue about something unrelated, they bring up the previous argument about the parking spot again.

Role ambiguity

If people aren't sure what they're supposed to do, they're likely to become frustrated and anxious. This makes conflict with others more likely. Also, if group members aren't clear which tasks they're supposed to be performing, the odds of people unintentionally working at cross purposes increases and this can cause conflict.

Role ambiguity typically causes feelings of possessiveness among employees. For example, an employee records on a whiteboard the things the group has to do every week. One day another employee decides to do the same. This could cause the first employee to become irritated, believing that someone else is trying to take over.

Task interdependency

Conflict is common when some members of a team depend on others to perform certain tasks before they can perform their own. This is mainly because dependency on others often causes anxiety and extra work pressure.

For example, one employee is tasked with arranging a company poster with a small write-up and lots of pictures.

The employee is given a week to do it. The employee finishes the write-up in two days, but has to wait for the company photographer to take pictures of the company building and staff. The employee can't finish the poster without the photos. If the photographer takes too much time, it is likely that a conflict will arise over the matter.

Take Raymond and Luke, who've been asked to work together to compile a sales report for their company's Accounts Department. Follow along as their conversation turns into a conflict.

Raymond: Hey, Luke. Have you had a chance to start looking for the figures for that report we've been given?

Luke: Um, no, not yet. I've been pretty busy doing other things.

Raymond: Other things? This is exactly what happened with the previous report I had to do with you. You say you're too busy, and I end up doing all the work by myself!

Raymond is surprised and angry.

Luke: What? I always do my fair share of work. And when I say I'm busy, it means I am. I can't stand working with you!

Luke is insulted and angry.

Question

Based on their conversation, what cause lies behind the conflict between Raymond and Luke?

Options:

1. Unresolved prior conflict
2. Role ambiguity
3. Task interdependency

Answer

Option 1: This is the correct option. The previous problem that Raymond and Luke had in working together was the basis for their new conflict.

Option 2: This option is incorrect. Raymond and Luke both knew what their own roles were in the task, so this wasn't the cause of the conflict between them.

Option 3: This option is incorrect. Although Raymond and Luke were working on the same task, neither of them had to wait for the other to complete work. So task interdependency wasn't the cause of the conflict.

Consider a group member who's responsible for editing the copy for an advertising campaign by a given deadline.

This person can't edit the copy until it has been written, despite pressure to get the work done. Also, if the copy is submitted late and it turns out that it is badly written and full of errors, the editor will have to work doubly hard at the last moment.

This type of situation often leads to conflict, and task interdependency is the cause. The editor's ability to complete a task properly depends on the actions of the writer, and this adds to the pressure on the editor.

The various causes of group conflict aren't mutually exclusive - often you'll find that more than one of these is involved in a particular conflict. For example, two members of a group had a conflict in the past and so are already slightly uncomfortable and mistrustful of one another. Then when their roles appear to overlap, open conflict is much more likely.

Question

John and Michael are tasked with organizing a business conference. During the initial planning meeting there is a heated debate about the venue for the conference, but eventually they reach an agreement.

John books the venue and waits for Michael to book a guest speaker before he can prepare and send invitations to the guests.

Michael also prepares a set of invitations and waits for John to book the guest speaker before he can send out his invitations.

An argument ensues when John and Michael discover that neither has booked a guest speaker, that each of them has created a set of invitations, but none have been sent to the guests.

What were main causes of the argument?

Options:

1. John and Michael didn't clarify their roles in organizing the conference and so ended up working at cross purposes and duplicating one another's efforts

2. John and Michael were both depending on each other to arrange a guest speaker before they could send out invitations

3. The heated debate John and Michael had during the initial planning meeting over the venue for the conference

4. An unresolved dispute between John and Michael over the budget for a previous project they worked on together

Answer

Option 1: This is a correct option. This is an example of role ambiguity because neither John nor Michael knew exactly which tasks they were responsible for.

Option 2: This option is correct. This is an example of task interdependency, because John and Michael were waiting for each other to perform a task – inviting a guest speaker – before they could send out invitations.

Option 3: This option is incorrect. This conflict was resolved and a venue was selected and booked.

Option 4: This option is incorrect. Without further information, it is unlikely that this unresolved conflict could be a cause of John and Michael's present argument.

Resolving group conflict

Conflict generally occurs in stages. First particular antecedents, or background circumstances, create the conditions for conflict. Next someone perceives a conflict and experiences associated tension, which in turn may motivate this person to take action to reduce the feelings of discomfort. The conflict then becomes open, potentially drawing in others. Finally, the conflict can be resolved only if everyone involved recognizes it and is willing to address it.

Once all the parties involved in a conflict are ready to address it, a manager can use a framework of five steps to help the parties resolve the conflict. The steps are to assess the situation, identify the source of the conflict, evaluate the personalities involved in the conflict, address each person's expectations, and finally determine an appropriate course of action.

1. Assess the situation

In the first step, the aim is to gather information about the situation causing the conflict. You can do this by asking questions to find out who's involved in the conflict, what the problem is, and how long the conflict has existed.

2. Identify source of conflict

The second step is to identify the source of the conflict. If you can understand its cause, you'll be better equipped to resolve it. You need to listen to each party involved in the conflict and identify any opposing goals or other causes that may have started the conflict.

3. Evaluate the personalities involved

The third step is to evaluate the personalities involved in the conflict. It's natural that not every type of person gets along with or understands every other type. You could already have a good idea of how each member typically behaves in various situations, but if not, past performance evaluations may be useful in providing background information about the individuals involved in a conflict.

4. Address expectations

The fourth step is to address expectations. It's important that all parties involved in the conflict have the same expectations of a possible resolution. This makes it possible to find a mutually beneficial solution that will allow the group to move forward.

5. Determine course of action

The fifth, and final, step is to determine a course of action that will resolve the conflict. It's important that all affected parties participate in choosing this course of action and agree that it represents the best alternative. It's also important to ensure the agreed action is carried out correctly and as agreed. All parties should be happy with the outcome. If they're not, the resolution process should be restarted.

Raymond and Luke have been continuing their argument and it has caught the attention of their manager, Julia, who calls them into her office. Follow along as Julia tries to resolve the conflict.

Julia: Hello, Raymond and Luke. Please come in and have a seat. I'm concerned that the two of you have been arguing and unable to work together over the past two days. What seems to be the problem?

Raymond: Morning, Julia. Well yes, it has been about two days now I suppose. I'm just finding it difficult to work with Luke. He's always saying that he's busy with other work when I ask him for something that needs to be done, like this report that's due tomorrow.

Julia: OK. Luke, why do you always seem so busy? Are you finding yourself overloaded with work?

Luke: Yes, actually I am. The director has been asking me to do quite a bit of extra work since his personal assistant resigned a couple of months ago. It has been taking up a lot of my time. I try to help Raymond out as much as I can when we're assigned something to work on together, but unfortunately it's not always possible..

Julia: As far as I can remember from both of your performance evaluations, neither of you two have experienced any problems with each other before. Luke, you're always up to date with your work and Raymond, you're known to work well with other people. So actually it's not clear which work should take priority. Is that right?

Luke: Yes, I don't like not being able to finish all of my work. I should have told Raymond before about all my extra work I have been receiving. From now on I'll try be more open about my work.

Julia: Hearing what Luke just said, what are your expectations now, Raymond?

Raymond: I expect Luke to tell me when he has extra work so we can prioritize better together. If I had known about the extra work in the first place, I wouldn't have overreacted like I did.

Julia: OK. It sounds like you both want the same things. Now let's try to figure out a solution to all this. Luke, would you agree to talk to the director about the extra work he's given you and how it's affecting your other work? If you'd like, I'll talk to him too and suggest that he find a replacement for his personal assistant.

Luke: Yes, I'll talk to him, and it would be great if you would too. Raymond: That sounds perfect to me. I'll also be more understanding now that

I know what pressure Luke is under.

Julia: Great. I'll go and speak to the director now.

Julia succeeds in resolving the conflict between Raymond and Luke. She progresses through all five of the steps. She first assesses the situation and identifies Luke's conflicting priorities as the source of the conflict. She considers the personalities involved, addresses Raymond and Luke's expectations, and finally participates with them in determining a suitable course of action.

Question

Sequence descriptions of the steps for resolving conflict between group members.

Options:

A. Gather as much information as possible about the conflict

B. Determine that ambiguity in group members' roles is the main cause of the conflict

C. Consider the characteristics of each person involved in the conflict

D. Speak to all parties about what they want and need in relation to addressing the conflict

E. Ensure all the affected parties collaborate in choosing an appropriate way to resolve the conflict

Answer

Gather as much information as possible about the conflict is ranked the first step. The first step is to assess the situation by asking questions to find out more about the conflict.

Determine that ambiguity in group members' roles is the main cause of the conflict is ranked the second step. The second step is to identify the source of the conflict so you can address this rather than just focusing on the "symptoms" of the conflict.

Consider the characteristics of each person involved in the conflict is ranked the third step. As a third step, you should evaluate the personalities of all the people involved in the conflict. This will help you determine the extent to which emotional conflict is playing a role, and equip you to guide everyone involved in working together.

Speak to all parties about what they want and need in relation to addressing the conflict is ranked the fourth step. As the fourth step, it's important to address everyone's expectations, determining what outcomes they require for the conflict to be resolved.

Ensure all the affected parties collaborate in choosing an appropriate way to resolve the conflict is ranked the fifth step. The final step in resolving conflict is to ensure that everyone involved participates in choosing an appropriate course of action for resolving the conflict.

CHAPTER 3 - Power and Politics

CHAPTER 3 - Power and Politics

Section 1 - Power in Organizations

Section 1 - Power in Organizations

Political interactions in the workplace are unavoidable. This is rooted in the fact that no organization is completely unified around singular goals. Adopting a political mindset in the workplace prepares you to navigate competing interests in ways that can benefit both you and your organization.

Five types of power may be exercised in organizations. These are legitimate, reward, coercive, expert, and referent power. Managers typically rely on legitimate, reward, and coercive power to influence subordinate employees, whereas colleagues rely mainly on expert, referent, and coercive power to influence one another.

The benefits of a political mindset

Many people feel that politics don't belong in the workplace. The unethical and untrustworthy image associated with many prominent politicians has certainly contributed to this. The reality, though, is that every organization is a system of political structures. You can try to ignore the politics in your organization. Or you can consciously adopt a political mindset that gives you the edge in navigating organizational politics.

At the most basic level, an organization is a group of people who work together. However, these people all have their own interests and aspirations. They also belong to different collections of groups, with interests that may compete. In this context, politics is the way that change is realized. It brings groups of people together, influencing them to work toward particular goals or do particular things. So it's what allows an organization to move forward.

Organizational politics can be defined as the activities and behaviors used for personal or organizational gain.

Depending on the assumptions you start with, you can interpret this definition in a negative or positive light.

The negative view is that organizational politics is divisive and self-serving, and generally bad for an organization.

In contrast, a more positive view is that individual and group interests can drive people to act in ways that benefit them and their organizations.

These perspectives are representative of two contrasting approaches to business organization – the rational organizational mindset and the political organizational mindset.

Rational organizational mindset

Those with a rational organizational mindset consider unity their priority. A shared focus on particular corporate goals becomes the basis for efficiency and effectiveness. Self-interest, and the competing interests of internal groups, are considered counterproductive. New initiatives and change processes are effected from the top down, with management at the various levels working to facilitate buy-in from employees.

Political organizational mindset

Those with a political organizational mindset prefer to focus on the constructive role that internal politics can play if it's managed correctly. They acknowledge the reality that all employees have their own interests, but believe that competing interests can be managed effectively for organizational benefit.

Effective leaders and employees don't hide from actively engaging in political interactions. They understand the benefits of embracing a political mindset and aim to navigate company politics in ways that will benefit them and their organizations. In addition to these, there are several other benefits to adopting a political mindset in the workplace:

- it can help you recognize and therefore avoid political traps that could damage or even ruin your career,
- it can equip you to protect yourself from organizational wrong-doing,
- it can assist you to develop skills that will benefit you personally in your career,
- it can help you make a difference to your organization that extends beyond your immediate sphere of influence, and
- it can help you adopt a more critical approach to your work, encouraging you to challenge assumptions, initiate change, and get results.

Question

What are the benefits of your having a political mindset in your organization?

Options:

1. You'll take a more critical approach to your work, which will enable you to get better results

2. You'll be able to avoid political situations that could ruin your career

3. You'll be able to focus on achieving your personal goals without being distracted by the company's vision

4. You'll be able to establish better friendships and spend more time with your colleagues

110

Answer

Option 1: This is a correct option. Adopting a political mindset enables you to take a more critical approach to your work – challenging assumptions, initiating change, and getting better results.

Option 2: This option is correct. Adopting a political mindset enables you to become more politically savvy and aware in the workplace. It can therefore help you prevent political relationships from compromising your career.

Option 3: This is an incorrect option. Adopting a political mindset should benefit both you and your organization. It's only possible to improve your position in an organization by ensuring your contribution impacts it positively.

Option 4: This option is incorrect. Although adopting a political mindset might serve to improve relationships in the workplace, this isn't always the result or its primary purpose. Increasing your effectiveness and ability to achieve objectives is the goal.

Power types

You need to be aware of the two important criteria for effectively navigating organizational politics. First you need to be able to recognize and understand the different types of power exercised in the workplace. Second, you need to identify what kind of powers you have and how to use the types effectively to get things done.

In business, power is the ability to get someone else to do something in order to obtain a desired result. So it's the ability to get things to happen in an intended way.

Influence is a closely related concept. It refers to the exercise of power. So the amount of influence you have depends, at least partly, on the amount of power you have.

Although many people have a negative perception of power, both power and influence can be used positively in the workplace. But because power can be abused very easily, using it in an organization requires caution.

The use of power in an organization can be positive only when it's rooted in a strong ethical foundation.

You need to be aware of the two important criteria for effectively navigating organizational politics. First you need to be able to recognize and understand the different types of power exercised in the workplace. Second, you need to identify what kind of powers you have and how to use the types effectively to get things done.

In business, power is the ability to get someone else to do something in order to obtain a desired result.

So it's the ability to get things to happen in an intended way.

Influence is a closely related concept. It refers to the exercise of power. So the amount of influence you have depends, at least partly, on the amount of power you have.

Although many people have a negative perception of power, both power and influence can be used positively in the workplace. But because power can be abused very easily, using it in an organization requires caution.

The use of power in an organization can be positive only when it's rooted in a strong ethical foundation.

Question

How would you describe your past experiences of politics, power, and influence in the workplace?

Options:

1. Mostly negative
2. A fair balance of positive and negative
3. Mostly positive

Answer

Option 1: Unfortunately, a negative experience with organizational politics is common to many people. Gaining a better understanding of the different types of power that are used in organizations will give you more insight into the dynamics at play and help you become more effective in achieving your objectives.

Option 2: You've experienced both sides of office politics in action and it would be easy for you to become disillusioned by focusing only on your negative experiences. Increasing your knowledge of the different types of power that are used in organizations will give you more insight into the dynamics at play and help you become more effective in achieving your objectives.

Option 3: You're fortunate to have been exposed to contexts in which organizational politics has been used in a healthy and productive manner. Increasing your understanding of the different types of power used in organizations will help you participate in organizational politics with even greater success.

An uneven distribution of power and influence is likely to exist among employees. Some may have more than others. There are also differences in the types of power that individuals possess.

To participate effectively in company politics, you must be able to recognize the different types of power and understand the various formal and informal factors that legitimize them.

Employees may exercise one or more of the five types of power in an organization:

- legitimate power,
- reward power,
- coercive power,

- expert power, and
- referent power.

Legitimate power, also known as formal power, is rooted in the degree of authority that accompanies a particular level in the organizational hierarchy. You hold legitimate power over another employee if you occupy a position of higher status. For example, managers hold legitimate power over the employees in their departments.

Say the managing director of an investments company decides to institute a more formal dress code policy for all employees. In this example, the managing director is exercising legitimate power, or formal authority, to impose a decision, irrespective of the opinions of those who are affected by it.

When an employee suggests that everyone pays a small fee to participate in casual day Friday, to raise money for popular charities, the managing director agrees to implement the idea.

This example doesn't involve exercising legitimate power because the managing director doesn't have the authority to force employees to donate money for charity or dress casually on Fridays.

Question

Which scenario best depicts the exercise of legitimate power?

Options:

1. A CEO postpones a meeting with departmental managers due to a conflict in her schedule

2. A CEO invites departmental managers to join him in celebrating his birthday with cake in his office

3. A CEO offers cash to a group of external auditors in return for a positive audit of his company

Answer

Option 1: This is the correct option. In this example, the CEO is drawing on her legitimate power, or formal authority, to impose a decision that her subordinates need to comply with, irrespective of their own opinions.

Option 2: This is an incorrect option. The managers can choose to accept or decline the CEO's invitation. It falls outside the CEO's authority to insist that they attend.

Option 3: This option is incorrect. In this example, the CEO is attempting to influence others, but he isn't drawing on the legitimate power associated with his position as a CEO to do this. Instead, he's trying to use the unethical – and in this case criminal – strategy of bribery to influence others.

Reward power is rooted in your capability to offer something desirable as a reward to others if they achieve specific outcomes. Rewards can be tangible, such as money, or intangible, such as praise.

For example, a manager can exercise tangible reward power by offering employees salary bonuses for attaining certain production goals.

Similarly, a sales manager could exercise intangible reward power by using the platform of a team meeting to publicly congratulate a sales agent who was last month's top sales performer.

Coercive power is the opposite of reward power. It depends on your ability to create fear by executing threats, administering discipline, or withholding rewards. Coercive power can be rooted in legitimate power or acquired through force and manipulation.

Rooted in legitimate power

When a manager issues a warning to an employee who has been consistently late for work, he's using coercive power that's rooted in legitimate power. The manager has a responsibility to exercise this power fairly and effectively to maximize employee performance.

Acquired through force and manipulation

A sales representative threatens to expose a colleague's abuse of sick leave unless the colleague gives him the names and contact numbers of his leads. This is an example of coercive power that's acquired through force and manipulation. It is highly unethical and can contribute to a negative atmosphere at work.

Expert power, also known as knowledge power, is based on a skill, ability, or information that you possess and others don't. It's particularly effective when others need your expertise to complete their own tasks or meet their objectives.

For example, when a salesperson's computer can't connect to the network, the salesperson calls a coworker from the IT Department. The salesperson is likely to follow the advice of the IT technician because that person has expert power.

People with charisma and personal magnetism hold referent power, also called charismatic power. It fosters a sense of admiration and trust in others, often making them more cooperative and easier to influence. For example, when a respected and well-liked manager proposes a resolution, which someone less popular opposes, others are more likely to give their support to the more popular manager.

You can use referent power over other employees to gain status, obtain help with tasks, or learn information that might be helpful to you in the workplace.

For example, a well-liked employee who asks questions is likely to be met with willing and friendly help – whereas someone generally unpopular is more likely to get irritated or rushed responses.

Charismatic power is strongly aligned with your social skills. Although you can't change your personality, making a conscious effort to develop your relationships with your coworkers can only serve to make your experience of the workplace more positive.

Question

Often employees can't continue with their work until the company's IT technician helps them address computer problems. The technician is always friendly and generally liked. He prioritizes any network- related technical problems, so employees often have to wait until he has the time to deal with their problems. They treat him with a high level of respect.

Which type of power is being exercised in this scenario?

Options:

1. Expert power
2. Referent power
3. Coercive power
4. Reward power

Answer

Option 1: This option is correct. Other employees depend on the IT technician's expertise to complete their own tasks. So his expertise is what gives him power over others.

Option 2: This is an incorrect option. Although the IT technician is friendly and well-liked, it's primarily his expertise that gives him power. Other employees depend on this expertise to get their jobs done.

Option 3: This option is incorrect. Colleagues respect the IT technician because he has expertise they need. He doesn't use coercive power, which would involve forcing employees to behave in certain ways. He doesn't resort to unethical means of gaining control over them and he has no legitimate authority to administer discipline or withhold rewards.

Option 4: This option is incorrect. The IT technician has no legitimate authority to offer rewards. Additionally, his position and responsibilities in the organization have no real connection to those of the employees he helps. As such, their performance levels have no bearing on him.

In an organization, the most common needs for using power are to obtain commitment, secure compliance, or overcome resistance.

An organization's formal hierarchy influences the types of power at each person's disposal.

Those in managerial positions are more likely to use legitimate and reward power to motivate employees to perform at desired levels. Managers may also have more opportunity to use coercive power, although this isn't a positive method of influence and isn't generally recommended.

Referent power and expert power come more into play as the criteria for power distribution between colleagues or employees at a similar level in an organization's formal hierarchy.

Colleagues may also use coercive power in the form of manipulation. It's ethically questionable, however, and you should aim to employ methods rooted in logic, friendship, and negotiation to influence the behavior of others. By reasoning with an individual or drawing on a friendship, you're more likely to persuade that person to help you meet your objectives.

Question

Match each power type to the scenario that most accurately depicts it.

Options:

A. Legitimate

B. Reward

C. Coercive

D. Expert

E. Referent

Targets:

1. A shop manager decides to extend operating times by two hours during the holiday season

2. To curb absenteeism, a company manager decides to compensate employees for unused sick days

3. To increase output, a CEO tells staff members that their jobs will be at risk if their performance doesn't improve

4. An agent at a real-estate office is a skillful photographer and his coworkers often ask him to help with photos for their own listings

5. The ideas of an extroverted and highly popular advertising representative are often favored over those of her colleagues

Answer

This is an example of the exercise of legitimate power. The manager can make decisions that affect all other employees because of the authority associated with the management position.

This is an example of the exercise of reward power. The manager is attempting to influence the behavior of employees through the prospect of a reward, in the form of financial compensation.

This is an example of the exercise of coercive power. The CEO is attempting to influence the behavior of staff by threatening them with negative consequences that will apply if their performance doesn't change.

This is an example of the exercise of expert power. The agent's skills as a photographer sets him apart from his coworkers and creates a relationship of dependence in which he has the power.

This is an example of the exercise of referent power. The advertising representative has power through her extroverted personality and popularity.

Section 2 - Organizational Politics

Section 2 - Organizational Politics

Positive political behavior benefits organizations without harming others, whereas negative political behavior is motivated by self-interest and has a potentially negative impact.

Negative political behaviors motivated by the desire to avoid action include overconforming to rules, passing responsibility, acting dumb, stretching tasks, and procrastinating – or dragging one's feet. Negative behaviors designed to avoid blame include obsessively documenting activities, avoiding negative situations, shifting blame, and misrepresenting facts.

Constructive political behavior is essential for effective leadership. Examples include continuously managing change, promoting worthwhile causes, seeking out like-minded individuals, accurately gauging the motives of others, using principled stealth, and networking within and outside an organization.

Examples of political behavior

Every workplace is a political arena and every individual takes part in or is affected by the power plays that occur. This politicking – or use of power in an attempt to achieve particular ends – is used for personal or organizational gain, and can be either positive or negative, depending on how it affects both individuals and the organization.

Positive

Positive politicking benefits an organization, even if the aim of the individual is personal gain. It involves promoting your own legitimate interests or organizational interests in a way that benefits the organization that doesn't violate ethical norms.

Examples of acceptable positive politicking include coaching others, working cooperatively with employees in other departments, and networking both within and outside the organization.

Negative

Negative political behaviors are usually motivated by self-interest. They don't benefit an organization and often violate ethical norms or boundaries.

Examples of negative political behavior are sabotaging employees or the organization in an underhanded way, starting malicious rumors, deliberately underperforming, and stealing from the workplace.

Negative politicking also often arises from employees' attempts to protect themselves. Examples are avoiding accountability for a mistake, dodging responsibility, taking credit for someone else's work, or protecting one's turf to the detriment of others.

Negative political behavior is most common in organizations where low levels of trust exist between management and employees, which in turn leads to poor morale.

This type of environment may have become the status quo in an organization or it might develop during periods of traumatic organizational change when there's uncertainty about the future.

Question

Match examples of behaviors to the appropriate categories. More than one example may match to a category.

Options:

A. Cooperating with a fellow employee to streamline interdepartmental work

B. Networking outside a company to promote the public events that have been organized this quarter

C. Taking paper from the photocopier each week to use in your printer at home

D. Speculating about your manager's personal life with a group of colleagues over morning coffee

Targets:

1. Politically positive
2. Politically negative

Answer

Cooperation and networking, both internally and externally, are examples of positive political behaviors that can benefit an organization.

Stealing from an organization and engaging in malicious gossip are negative political behaviors – they're driven by self-interest and have potentially negative effects on an organization.

Negative political behavior

Negative political behaviors in an organization usually fall into one of two main categories – avoiding action or avoiding blame.

Both types of negative political behaviors can increase tension between individuals and groups, cripple decision making, and hamper organizational change.

If these behaviors become widespread and persistent, a negative political culture prevails which can easily lead to organizational stagnation.

A variety of political behaviors may help employees avoid having to take action – or enable those employees to get away with doing as little as possible within the confines of their jobs. Examples of these behaviors, which can cost an organization dearly, happen when employees overconform to rules, pass responsibility on to someone else, act dumb, stretch tasks, and procrastinate.

Over-conform

Over-conforming to rules involves strict, bureaucratic adherence to formal rules as a technique for avoiding action.

For example, employees may argue that particular tasks fall outside their authority or outside the scope of their departments' responsibilities as a strategy for avoiding the tasks.

Pass responsibility

Passing responsibility on to someone else involves making the completion of a job – or its outcome – someone else's problem.

For example, an employee who's drafted a report may refer all questions to a more senior person, stating that this person is responsible for addressing all queries.

Act dumb

Acting dumb involves feigning ignorance or a lack of required skills as a technique for avoiding particular tasks.

For instance, it's easy for an unwilling employee to say, "I don't know the process" or "I don't know how to use that software" to convince a manager or colleague that someone else should be asked to complete the work.

Stretch tasks

The tendency to stretch short tasks to fit generous time frames is a phenomenon in offices everywhere. Often employees prolong tasks as far as possible to avoid being assigned new work.

For example, an employee may perform an assigned task as slowly as possible, redoing parts of the work, discussing it with colleagues, and taking long breaks, to avoid being assigned a new task.

Procrastinate

127

Employees who procrastinate may at first seem willing to take on a task or support a project or proposal, but then fail to back up the verbal agreement with timely action. Like stretching tasks, it involves wasting time. It can also take the form of passive resistance, which involves wilfully doing the barest minimum work required out of spite toward an employer. Passive resistance is particularly difficult to address directly.

Suppose a software development company introduced the practice of having two managers check all junior employees' work in coding projects after a few avoidable mistakes weren't corrected before the product was presented to the client. After some weeks, the practice simply fell away because coders had become aware of how not to make the same mistakes and managers simply didn't have the time to implement the practice on an on-going basis.

However, because managers never officially put an end to the practice, one front-end coder keeps insisting that his managers must check his work before passing it on to the next step of production. The managers are currently very busy, so this results in long delays.

This is an obvious example of over-conformance to a rule. It's also a directly political behavior if the employee knows it will help him avoid extra work, or is using it as a strategy to passively resist the authority that the organization has over him.

Question

A colleague works in the warehouse, collating stock. You know she doesn't enjoy her job and is just sticking it out until she manages to find another position. She frequently leaves her work half done, knowing that her team leader is compelled to finish it for her. Also, whenever others have a question related to the company's inventory, she directs them to her team leader.

Which type of negative political behavior is this colleague demonstrating?

Options:

1. Over-conforming to rules
2. Passing responsibility
3. Acting dumb
4. Stretching tasks

Answer

Option 1: This is an incorrect option. The employee in this example isn't adhering to particular rules, or using rules as the basis for shirking her responsibilities.

Option 2: This is the correct option. The employee in this scenario is avoiding work and accountability by passing her responsibilities to her team leader.

Option 3: This option is incorrect. Although the employee in this example refers anyone with questions to her team leader, she doesn't directly pretend not to have the knowledge or skills required to complete particular tasks.

Option 4: This option is incorrect. The employee in this case isn't stretching her tasks so that they take longer to complete. She simply isn't completing her tasks and she's passing the responsibility for them to her team leader.

The second category of negative political behavior involves avoiding blame. It's inevitable that sometimes people make mistakes or that initiatives have undesirable outcomes. People may go to considerable lengths to protect themselves from the fallout. For example, they could rigorously document activities, completely avoid potentially negative situations, shift blame to others, and misrepresent the facts.

Rigorously document activities

Employees who rigorously document their activities can give the illusion of competence and attention to detail, even if their real intent is to protect themselves from blame. When things go wrong, it's easy for these employees to cast aspersions on others who haven't meticulously recorded details of all their actions.

This type of behavior is similar in some ways to over-conforming to rules because it involves being overly bureaucratic.

Avoid negative situations

Individuals may actively avoid potentially negative situations and attempt only projects or tasks where success is likely. This doesn't necessarily hurt others, but it can result in employees being far less productive and competent than they could otherwise be. Also, employees who maneuver politically to ensure they're assigned only tasks that will enhance their success may prevent their colleagues from participating in these tasks. This will reduce the colleagues' chances of furthering their careers.

Shift blame

A common strategy for avoiding blame is to shift the blame onto someone or something else. Often the people blamed aren't available to defend themselves. Examples are blaming a person who's no longer with the company or even blaming a poor fiscal year for the failure of a project.

Misrepresent facts

Employees may avoid blame by misrepresenting facts to cast their own actions in a positive light – sometimes at the direct expense of others – or to omit anything potentially damning.

A lot of politicking involves portraying the truth in a favorable way. However, misrepresenting facts involves direct manipulation of the truth, either through lying or the omission of relevant facts.

In a bank, suppose two of your colleagues both document all the work-related tasks they perform.

One of these colleagues uses her records to improve her time management. She makes sure that recording details of her activities never interferes with her work. Her actions have potentially positive effects, for her and her organization.

The other colleague spends a lot of his actual work time documenting his activities to account for his time, in case he's ever questioned about his efficiency. He slightly inflates the duration of each task he performs. This employee is acting entirely out of self-interest, and his behavior has a negative effect on the organization.

Another colleague works in the Customer Relations Department. He's part of a team that deals with complaints. He has a habit of sifting through recorded complaints and choosing to deal only with ones that he knows will be easy to resolve. His tendency to avoid negative situations might give him the appearance of competency, but it means that only more difficult complaints are left for his peers to handle.

In rare cases when a customer's complaint can't be resolved successfully, the same employee always finds someone or something else to blame. For example, he shifts the blame for an administrative error to the bank's computing system.

On another occasion, he blames the IT Department for failing to provide a customer with assistance, when in fact he hasn't alerted the department to the customer's problem.

Almost all examples of negative political behaviors are motivated by self-interest or self-protection. Unfortunately, they also often involve hurting others – and they can compromise the overall success of an organization.

Question

Match each type of negative behavior to the appropriate category. More than one example may match to a category.

Options:

A. An employee records minute details of how he spends his time each day, in case his efficiency is questioned

B. A manager goes to great lengths to ensure she's awarded only projects for which the risks are low

C. An employee follows an outdated process outlined in a company handbook as a strategy for slowing down his work

D. A graphic designer pretends not to know how to optimize a set of graphics so the task is given to someone else

Targets:

1. Avoiding blame
2. Avoiding action

Answer

Employees may seek to avoid blame by rigorously documenting activities. They may also avoid risks in an attempt to avoid blame in case anything goes wrong.

Over-conforming to the rules of a company can count as negative political behavior when it's used as a way to avoid work. Acting dumb by pretending not to have the required skills to perform a task is another type of avoiding action.

Constructive political leadership

In any organization, individuals and groups have different interests – but it's necessary to bring people together if they're to support common, organizational goals. So leaders in an organization must be politically savvy – and use various types of positive political behavior – if they're to overcome various types of political resistance to their ideas and goals.

A politically savvy leader has a good understanding of political relationships in an organization, and can recognize and counter negative political resistance.

Such a leader recognizes all the different obstacles in the way of a good idea and identifies appropriate tactics for navigating past those obstacles.

Take the simple example of a team leader trying to get her supervisor and her team members to adopt an innovative new process.

134

The manager has to make it clear how the process will benefit everyone whose support she needs if her idea is to get the go-ahead and be implemented successfully. So without tangible, formal benefits like pay raises to offer to all the players involved, she needs to use clever politicking to get everyone's support.

Leaders can use a variety of behaviors in politically constructive ways that benefit them and their organizations. They can continuously manage change, promote worthwhile causes, seek out like- minded individuals, and gauge the responses and attitudes of others accurately. They can also use stealth in a principled manner, and develop their internal and external support network.

Continuously manage change

Organizational change is a business constant, which management usually steers to improve business. This state of change is in addition to regular office work. Politically savvy managers must consider continuous change management as a permanent part of their jobs. For example, they may regularly review work methods with their teams.

Promote worthwhile causes

For managers to achieve their organizational goals, they need to negotiate and maneuver with various others to have that goal championed. One way to accomplish this is to enthusiastically promote worthwhile causes that are supported by or will benefit others. This also includes giving recognition and support to the causes of others if they will be beneficial.

An example of this would be a manager promoting an initiative, such as a switch to a new company health insurance scheme, before it's formally sanctioned to gain support for it.

Seek out like-minded individuals

When promoting worthwhile causes, politically savvy managers will seek out like-minded individuals to give the cause support. This is especially useful when dealing with immediate or local interests. By establishing a group willing to work toward a goal – whether it's a formal group like a team or department, or simply a collection of individuals with similar aims, a manager can direct the work in the necessary direction.

Gauge others accurately

In a complex political arena, the goals and abilities of others are not always clear. It's important for a political manager to know who will support or oppose them, and what influence those individuals can exert. This includes understanding the motives and political awareness of allies and detractors and can most effectively be achieved by interpersonal communication.

Use stealth

Effective managers operate within formal organizational rules, but can push the boundaries when necessary. This includes a principled use of stealth to further political aims. This can include activities like selectively withholding information from others and obscuring the motive behind fostering a political alliance. These differ from misrepresenting the facts by virtue that the goal is beneficial to the organization, not the individual.

Develop internal and external network

Forging beneficial professional relationships is an important part of being a politically savvy leader, and is accomplished through internal and external networking. To find allies and supporters, a leader must take every opportunity to engage with others, inside and outside an organization, and to determine shared goals or ways in which acquaintances can be mutually beneficial. Increasingly, relationships outside of an organization are being considered important in allowing people to share resources, ideas, and projects.

Curtis is the marketing manager at the branch of a nationwide advertising agency.

He works in a fast-paced business, and work processes change constantly to keep up with new trends and technology. Curtis frames this continuous change management as part of his daily duties, conveying this to his team through meetings and training sessions where necessary.

By making organizational change a cornerstone of his job, he's able to cope with shifts in organizational interests and goals, realigning his team's efforts as and when necessary.

Curtis wants to establish a greater bond between his team and the company's Art Department because this will streamline the processes of both parties. However, different people in the top ranks of management run the Art and Marketing Departments.

As a result of his internal networking, he has allies in the Art Department who support his ideas.

His strategy to get the teams to work more closely together relies on enough supporters in both camps, so that more casual, quicker channels of communication can be established. To start his endeavor, he meets informally and discreetly with his allies. So he uses principled stealth until he has positive results he can present to top-ranking management.

When Curtis has tangible evidence to deliver to top management to prove the benefits of his endeavor, he must first gauge the motives of those he approaches, so he can start with the person most receptive to his idea and hence most likely to give support.

Once the new initiative is in place, and unnecessary steps in the interdepartmental communications process have been removed, it's evident how Curtis used his political maneuvering to garner support and take steps to affect organizational change.

Curtis's use of politics is positive and constructive because it benefits his organization without causing harm to any individuals or groups.

Question

Which actions are typical of politically constructive organizational leaders?

Options:

1. Promote ideas that are beneficial to the organization and individuals

2. Use moderate subterfuge when absolutely necessary in the pursuit of organizational gain

3. Establish political connections with others inside and outside the organization

4. Use interpersonal interactions to determine the motives of others

5. Use subterfuge to exclude others from a project in order to claim all the credit

6. Take steps to prevent changes to existing processes and procedures, to ensure stability

Answer

Option 1: This option is correct. Promoting worthwhile causes that elicit support is typical of a constructive leader.

Option 2: This is a correct option. The principled use of stealth is acceptable for a constructive leader as long as it benefits the organization.

Option 3: This option is correct. Effective leaders recognize the need for and benefits of both internal and external networking.

Option 4: This is a correct option. If you're to be an effective leader, it's important that you can gauge the motives and abilities of others to determine whether they'll support or oppose you.

Option 5: This option is incorrect. Constructive leaders use stealthy maneuvering only in an ethical way, for the benefit of their organizations.

Option 6: This is an incorrect option. Constructive leaders incorporate continual change management in their duties. They recognize that change is inevitable and are adept at adapting to it.

Section 3 - Leveraging Politics in Leadership

Section 3 - Leveraging Politics in Leadership

Leaders can use a variety of constructive actions to promote support for particular courses of action. These include making inspirational and personal appeals, consulting with peers, making exchanges, using rational persuasion, creating coalitions, and securing the endorsement of an expert or trusted figure.

An effective leader inspires employees to want to achieve organizational goals. Tactics for doing this include presenting employees with a vision of a bright future, creating a sense of urgency, offering rewards, having a reputation for delivering the goods, working with passion, and demonstrating care for employees.

Promoting a course of action

Given that individual employees have their own interests, how do leaders get things done in an organization? To do this, they need to use various power tactics to make sure their messages are understood and acted upon. They also need to be able to inspire people to act and to lead them with enthusiasm.

A constructive political leader is adept at getting others to work toward goals and to follow particular courses of action. Among the actions a leader can use to do this are making inspirational and personal appeals, using consultation, making exchanges, using rational persuasion, forming coalitions, and using expert consultation.

Inspirational appeals

Inspirational appeals are requests that play on employees' emotions, values, or sense of pride, and boost belief in a given course of action. They're often used to rally support.

Personal appeals

Making personal appeals involves calling on individuals for their support, often because you already have their friendship and personal loyalty.

Consultation

Consulting with others makes them feel involved and helps secure their buy-in for a particular course of action. It gives them a vested interest in the action.

Exchanges

Making exchanges involves making trades to secure the support or outcomes you want. Sometimes leaders also preempt an exchange by doing favors for others, who then feel bound to reciprocate at a later time.

Rational persuasion

Using rational persuasion involves giving good, logical reasons as to why a particular course of action will succeed, in order to gain support for it.

Coalitions

Creating coalitions involves forming groups of people – usually consisting of your peers – who may have different interests but support the particular course of action you want to propose.

Expert consultation

Expert consultation involves having an expert in a relevant field – or someone with experience and whose opinions are respected – endorse a course of action you're promoting, in order to influence others.

Zach is the manager of a research team at a pharmaceuticals company that specializes in medicines for treating muscular conditions and injuries.

He's determined to send Libby, who's one of his top researchers, to an important overseas conference focusing on sports medicine. He feels the conference represents a fantastic networking opportunity, as well as a chance to learn from a variety of top scientists who'll be offering talks and workshops on new developments in the field.

The drawback is the expense. Also, Libby is extremely busy with an existing project, and some top managers are already opposed to the idea.

Zach's plan involves creating a presentation to demonstrate the knowledge benefits to his department, and how these would enable the creation of a potentially lucrative new line of products. He needs the support of his own team, the Accounts Department, other managers, and if possible, experts in the field of sports medicine. Because his idea hasn't yet been formally sanctioned, he'll need to rely on his leadership tactics to convince the relevant parties to get their support.

Zach first approaches the members of his own team. He'll need them to collaborate to compile information and photographs for the presentation.

Zach explains that the team is already considered the top research unit in the company, and that the honor of sending one of its members to a prestigious, international conference is a possibility. Such an achievement would reflect positively on everyone in the team.

Zach's enthusiasm is infectious, and members of the team agree to put in extra work to create an impressive presentation. His inspirational appeal speaks to team members' sense of pride in their work and their hunger for further achievements.

Zach then needs to get support from the leader of another team, Shirley. He also wants to ask his friend in accounting, Patrick, to compile a report projecting profits if the new information from the conference is used to create new products. And he wants to ask Nigel, a specialized researcher from another team, to draw up a report specifying how the new information can be used to create the products. Zach has a different formal relationship with each potential ally and must therefore use the appropriate technique to achieve his goals.

Shirley

As the leader of another department, Shirley has excellent organizational skills and experience. Zach asks Shirley to help him put together a plan for the proposed trip, including which workshops and meetings to attend for maximum benefits. Shirley runs her own department, but she's able to recognize the plan's benefit and agrees to help.

Shirley is Zach's peer. He gains her support through consultation. Shirley may not benefit directly from the conference, but being involved in planning Zach's initiative gives her a vested interest in its success.

Patrick

Although Patrick works in accounting and doesn't work directly with Zach, they are friends outside of work. Zach makes a personal appeal to Patrick for help, relying on Patrick's loyalty and friendship to secure his help.

Patrick gladly agrees to spend some time creating the report, although this falls outside his usual responsibilities. He knows that in turn, he can rely on Zach for help if and when he needs it.

Nigel

Although Nigel is a junior employee and doesn't work on Zach's team, Zach knows that Nigel is the researcher best suited to writing a proposal for potential new products. So Zach suggests an exchange – he promises to support Nigel's application for the position of a research team leader, in return for the time Nigel spends creating a proposal. So Zach helps Nigel advance his career in return for his support.

Question

Which actions can a leader take to promote a particular course of action?

Options:

1. Inspire people to get their support
2. Offer to give something in return for people's support
3. Involve people in planning the action
4. Create a false impression that the action is already supported by top managers
5. Threaten people with formal disciplinary action if they don't provide their support
6. Call on support from friends and allies

Answer

Option 1: This option is correct. Making an inspirational appeal can garner support for a proposed course of action.

Option 2: This is a correct option. A leader can offer an exchange to secure needed support or help from others.

Option 3: This option is correct. Involving others in planning a course of action gives them a vested interest in its success.

Option 4: This option is incorrect. A constructive leader wouldn't misrepresent the facts to garner support for a plan.

Option 5: This is an incorrect option. Threatening people isn't a good way to obtain their support – and it may involve abusing a leadership position.

Option 6: This option is correct. A constructive leader may make personal appeals to garner support or help from friends and loyal allies.

Zach knows that it's vital to get support for his initiative from a high-ranking executive. He schedules a meeting with one of the company's managing directors.

In the meeting, Zach uses solid projections and figures from the reports to back up his business case for the conference and possible new product line. His enthusiasm shows, but it's on logical argument that he relies.

So it's through rational persuasion that Zach gains the executive's support.

Zach also does some scouting and determines which other team leaders are likely to support the creation of new product lines. He e-mails these team leaders, informing them of his plan and asking for their support.

The group of team leaders will have little effect on the decision about whether to send Libby to the conference, but represents an important support base for Zach. In future, he may be able to exert influence through the group.

Zach has established this coalition not just to lend support for his current plan, but to participate in supporting future courses of action that may stem from the conference.

Next Zach contacts a retired chemist who still consults for the pharmaceutical company and who's widely regarded as the best chemist the company has ever worked with. He's respected by all the company's organizational leaders. Zach e-mails his proposal and the backing projections to the chemist, and asks for his support.

The chemist agrees that the suggested new line could certainly be successful. Although he lacks formal authority in the company, his word can influence those who make the final decisions. Zach knows this will positively affect people's support for his initiative.

As a final step, Zach elicits the help and advice of various experts in the company. Together with his other actions, his use of expert consultation helps ensure support for his proposed course of action.

Zach was lucky to get support from all the parties he approached, but this won't always be the case. Types of responses you can expect to political leadership tactics range from commitment, to compliance or resistance.

Commitment

People who commit to a particular course of action support it fully and with enthusiasm.

Compliance

People who merely comply are willing to support an action, but without much fervor or enthusiasm. They're unlikely to put a lot of effort into providing assistance.

Resistance

Resistance comes from people who actively oppose a course of action you attempt to promote.

Question

Which are examples of constructive actions a leader can take to promote a course of action?

Options:

1. Use a reputable expert's endorsement to convince others of the action's merits

2. State the logical benefits of the course of action

3. Exaggerate the benefits of the action while pitching it to peers

4. Form a group of allies with similar goals who support the action

5. Tie employees' support for the action to performance-related bonuses

Answer

Option 1: This is a correct option. A constructive leader can consult a trusted expert whose word carries weight in order to garner support.

Option 2: This option is correct. A constructive leader should use rational persuasion to influence others to support a course of action.

Option 3: This is an incorrect option. A constructive leader would state only the actual benefits of a course of action, or risk losing the respect and cooperation of others.

Option 4: This is a correct option. Forming a coalition can provide support for a course of action.

Option 5: This is an incorrect option. Such a course of action could easily lead to resentment among employees and eventual loss of support.

Getting the best from employees

Constructive organizational politics is about more than simply influencing others to support occasional initiatives. The best possible case for the constructive politician isn't simply to get employees to achieve goals, but to change minds and behavior and align employee and organizational goals. Ideally, employees should want to achieve company goals.

Leaders can use various techniques to secure the buy-in of employees to organizational goals. You can present employees with a vision of a bright future, create a sense of urgency, offer rewards, deliver results, work with passion, and care for your employees.

Present a bright future

If you determine what employees value, you can tie those values to organizational goals and present a bright future. If you can present work aims as a way to achieve acceptance from peers, a way to do something meaningful, or a way to achieve belonging, for example, it's likely you'll inspire people.

Create a sense of urgency

You can motivate employees to perform if you create a sense of urgency about their work. If you can use statistics or facts to get people emotionally charged about their jobs, you can make them more proactive.

Offer rewards

One way to motivate employees is by offering them rewards. However, a reward system usually produces only temporary results – and rewards of ever increasing value are required if they're to keep motivating improved performance. So although rewards are the basis of paid employment, they're not that effective. An appeal to values is a more effective way to make a permanent change to an employee's attitude.

Deliver results

If you can maintain a reputation that you always deliver the results, people will be more inclined to follow your lead. A reliable leader who carries every plan through to completion will command loyalty and set an example that employees will gladly follow.

Work with passion

Leaders who exude enthusiasm and positive energy will go a long way in motivating employees and changing attitudes. If you do your work with passion, you'll inspire others and secure their support.

Care for employees

People generally respond better to care, appreciation, and respect than to coercion or threats. If you can demonstrate care for your employees and take time to build strong relationships with them, you'll win trust and support – for yourself and the goals you're working to achieve.

Glen is a manager in a small-town Parks Department and is heading a beautification drive for the derelict park in the town center. The project involves getting the park cleaned up, planting new flora, organizing the launch function, setting up a municipal presence online, and preventing the park facilities from sliding into disrepair again. Although Glen has formal authority, his employees are already overworked and are picky about which causes they support with enthusiasm.

Glen needs to get a huge amount of work out of his team to get all the tasks completed in time. He needs his team to oversee an effort to clean the park, design the park department web site and launch it before the park opens, organize for a local school to paint a mural on a graffiti-covered park wall, and canvas the area to get local business support. With such a volume of work, Glen will need his team enthusiastic and happy to work on weekends for at least two months before the opening.

Clean park

Glen knows that many people in his department live near the park, so he's able to present a bright future of a beautified neighborhood that residents can be proud of. This inspires his team to take an active role in managing the group of workers Glen organizes to clean the park.

Design web site

Glen needs the Parks Department to publicize the project online and establish an interactive page to let residents communicate with the municipality. To create a sense of urgency and get his team to be enthusiastic about designing the web site and writing copy, he explains that the web site will be unveiled during a grand opening and that the mayor and town councilors will test the site.

Organize mural

Glen wants a local school's Art Department to decorate a dirty park wall with an uplifting mural. Glen knows that one of his employees has an artistic son who often organizes creative events at his school. Glen can offer rewards in exchange for the school's participation – he gives his employee the opportunity for her son's artwork to be displayed in the park and he gives the school the opportunity to become involved in a future social upliftment project.

Get local business support

Glen asks two members of his department who are known in the community to help him get local business buy-in for the project, in terms of limited sponsorship and simply taking an active interest in the maintenance of the park. Despite the fact that the team is already working hard, Glen does his share of the canvassing with such passion that he inspires the two team members to tackle their respective tasks with equal enthusiasm.

Work weekends

Glen knows this project will require him and his team to work weekends for at least two months before the park's opening. His team is inspired by Glen's reputation for being someone who always delivers the results he promises and its members want to uphold Glen's and, by association, the team's good reputation.

As well as Glen's determination, enthusiasm, and hard work, he demonstrates care for his employees. He treats his employees with respect and compassion.

When the rush for the opening event is over, Glen makes sure that members of his team all receive a couple of days off to recover. He doesn't promise the leave up front, so it doesn't constitute a reward offered in return for work.

Glen manages to coordinate a successful project involving various tasks and a lot of overtime work. As a constructive leader, he never uses threats or fear as a motivator. Instead, he relies on positive leadership techniques to inspire his team to work toward their goal.

Question

Which tactics can leaders use to get the best from employees?

Options:

1. Establish a system to scare employees who don't perform at their best

2. Create a positive image of the impact of an employee's work

3. Lead by example and tackle work with enthusiasm

4. Give compelling reasons why tasks need to be tackled with urgency

5. Never complain if employees make mistakes or fail to deliver work to ensure their popularity

Answer

Option 1: This option is incorrect. Coercion and threats are unlikely to motivate employees over the long term.

Option 2: This is a correct option. An effective leader inspires people to work toward organizational goals by providing them with an image of the bright future their work can create.

Option 3: This option is correct. An effective leader inspires others by demonstrating passion and commitment.

Option 4: This is a correct option. One of the ways a constructive leader can motivate employees to work harder and support goals is by creating a sense of urgency about their work.

Option 5: This option is incorrect. The aim of constructive leaders isn't simply to be well-liked – it's to motivate employees to work well and to support organizational goals.

CHAPTER 4 - Structure and Employee Behavior

CHAPTER 4 - Structure and Employee Behavior

Section 1 - Organization Structures and Behavior

Section 1 - Organization Structures and Behavior

Organizational structure refers to the way jobs in an organization are formally divided, grouped, and coordinated. This directly affects employee behavior.

Defining elements of an organizational structure include degree of specialization, staff division, centralization, standardization of rules, chain of authority, and the extent of managers' control.

Types of organizational structures include functional, divisional, and matrix structures. Each has specific advantages and disadvantages.

Importance of organizational structure

Have you ever looked inside a PC? It may look like a jumble of chips, circuit boards, and wires, but a professional understands how the parts work together as a whole to make a functioning computer. If the components aren't correctly structured, performance suffers or the computer may not work at all. Organizations are similar – those with appropriate structures provide a productive and efficient work environment, with motivated employees and satisfied customers.

Organizational structure refers to the way jobs in an organization are formally divided, grouped, and coordinated. Every organization has a definitive structure that serves as the blueprint for how it functions.

Elements of organizational structure, such as the division of tasks among employees and the level of supervision each employee has, affect employees' behavior.

Organizational structure shouldn't be confused with organizational design, which refers to how the elements of organizational structure are integrated and managed.

Organizations can be roughly categorized as having organizational structures that are either flat or hierarchical. Each type of structure has particular characteristics that affect the behavior of employees.

Flat

Organizations with flat structures are more democratic than those with hierarchical structures. There's a greater level of communication, both up and down the chain of authority, and employees are encouraged to give feedback.

In an example of a flat organizational chart, a hierarchy includes only three levels. A CEO occupies the top position. Departmental directors are included in a row below the CEO, and other employees are included in a row below the directors.

Hierarchical

An organization with a hierarchical structure has a steeper hierarchy, with a tight chain of authority. Orders filter down from the top and employees are typically expected to complete tasks without question. This is the usual structure among large organizations.

In an example of a hierarchical organizational chart, a hierarchy includes seven levels – with a CEO at the top and then a vice president, departmental directors, assistant directors, team leaders, senior employees, and finally junior employees.

An organizational chart doesn't fully illustrate all the subtleties of an organizational structure. However, it gives a representation of its internal workings and of employees' relative positions in the chain of authority.

An organization's structure may be designed or it may evolve as an organization develops. Either way, it should ensure consistency in operations and employee relationships, and enable an organization to run as smoothly as possible. Efficient organizational structures promote positive and productive behavior. They motivate employees and boost performance by clarifying the purpose of every task.

Say a bank employee spends each day calling clients to ensure they are happy with the home loan service they received. In itself, this task may be repetitive and potentially tedious.

However, the task is more inspiring if it's seen in the context of the full process for enabling customers to purchase homes, and of continually improving that process based on customer feedback.

If an organizational structure works efficiently, the end result of any task is easy to see, and every person within that structure will feel some responsibility for an organization's overall results.

Elements of organizational structure

Various elements of organizational structure affect employees' behavior. These include specialization, staff division, centralization, the standardization of rules, chain of authority, and extent of control.

Specialization

Specialization refers to the way that tasks are split into multiple jobs and allocated to employees. In a highly specialized organization, each employee works on a single aspect of a task.

For example, an employee in a factory assembly line who adds a specific plastic component to computer monitors has a highly specialized job. On the other hand, a grade school teacher who teaches several subjects has a job with low specialization.

Staff division

Staff division is the way that employees are grouped. Usually this is by relativity – meaning that employees doing the same or similar tasks are identified as groups.

For example, a newspaper may divides its employees into staff writers, photographers, editorial staff, advertising salespeople, and accounts staff.

Centralization

Centralization refers to concentrating decision-making power in a small number of individuals. Decentralized organizations, on the other hand, spread decision-making power through a hierarchy of executives, supervisors, and managers.

A company is highly centralized if, for example, every decision must be checked and approved by the company owner or director.

Standardization

Standardization is the process of achieving consistency in the treatment of all employees and in business practices. For instance, job descriptions, procedures for completing tasks, and attendance policies help ensure standardization.

An example of a highly standardized organization is a factory where every employee clocks in at the same time, takes regulated coffee and lunch breaks, and ends work at the same time.

Chain of authority

The chain of authority is the formal hierarchy of an organization that determines which individuals have authority over others. If there's a clearly defined chain of authority, every employee reports to only one person.

An example of a strict chain of authority would be a salesperson reporting to an immediate supervisor, but never communicating with anyone further up in the organizational hierarchy.

Extent of control

The extent of a manager's control is measured by how many employees the manager supervises. A manager who supervises 20 people has a wider extent of control than a manager who supervises only 5 people, for example.

Often organizations give their managers wider extents of control to reduce the number of levels in their organizational hierarchies. This can reduce the numbers of employees needed and so save money.

Specialization can increase an organization's efficiency by eliminating the time required to shift mentally from doing one task to another.

However, the repetition of highly specialized jobs can result in boredom and frustration for employees. So it's important to find a balance between specialization and variety in the tasks employees perform.

There are two main types of specialization – vertical and horizontal.

Vertical

Vertical specialization occurs most in organizations with hierarchical organizational structures. It involves dividing tasks into jobs based on the level of authority they require. Tasks that involve making important decisions, for example, are divided among jobs at the top of the organizational hierarchy.

Horizontal

Horizontal specialization involves dividing tasks into jobs laterally, based on criteria other than the level of authority they require. Some organizations choose to move some decision- making authority down the hierarchy to encourage employee participation in organizational processes.

Although staff division by relativity is common, staff can also be divided into groups by products, by markets, or by location. For example, an automotive manufacturer might create separate staff divisions for each of the main types of vehicles it produces or for each of the geographical regions it serves. Or it may group staff based on the locations of the branches where they work.

A high degree of staff division can enhance communication between members of each group, but it may hinder communication between the groups.

Like with staff division, it's important to find the right balance between centralization and decentralization. The modern trend is toward decentralization, with organizations focusing on the use of internally driven departments and flexible teams authorized to make their own decisions.

However, extreme decentralization can hamper productivity. Unless all the departments and teams authorized to make decisions communicate well with one another, it can lead to duplicated effort, jobs left unfinished, and internal conflict.

When determining the appropriate level of standardization, it's important to consider individual personalities and needs.

Some employees may thrive when given high levels of independence, while others perform better with a more rigid, standardized structure.

Chains of authority in organizations have become less formal than in previous generations.

Although some organizations still enforce strict chains of authority, others encourage employees to communicate with higher-level management and executives. This can save time and help employees work more efficiently.

Giving managers wider spans of control can help managers make decisions more effectively, as well as reducing costs.

However, wide extents of control are effective only when employees are comfortable with their jobs and coworkers.

Question

Match each element of organizational structure to the appropriate example.

Options:

A. Specialization

B. Staff division

C. Centralization

D. Standardization

E. Chain of authority

F. Extent of control

Targets:

1. An employee's only task is fitting lenses into cell phone cameras

2. Employees working on a particular advertising campaign are grouped in the same office

3. A managing director has to approve any strategic decisions before they're implemented

4. A business that requires each employee to undergo an annual physical check-up

5. A designer in an advertising agency is expected to report any problems directly to a supervisor, who then reports them to an art director

6. A team leader oversees a team of 11 people

Answer

In an organization with a high degree of specialization, employees often work solely on a single aspect of a task.

Staff division is the way that employees are grouped – for example, by relativity, product, market, or location.

Centralization refers to the concentration of decision-making power in one or a small number of people.

Standardization of rules provides consistency in employee treatment and business practices. An example is a company's rules regarding physical health exams.

The chain of authority determines which individuals have authority over others, as well as determining reporting relationships.

Extent of control refers to the number of employees a manager or leader supervises.

Organizational structures

Every organization is unique, with its own distinctive combinations of people, processes, products, and customers. So no one organizational structure is always the best. Instead, it's important to develop a structure that meets an organization's particular needs.

Large organizations may have organizational structures that include substructures of different types or they may have completely different types of structures within their various operating divisions.

This can be effective provided that the structures work together as a cohesive whole.

There are various types of organizational structures, each made up of a particular combination of structural elements. Among the main types are functional, divisional, and matrix structures.

Functional

Functional organizational structures group employees by task, and are the simplest and most common. They include a low degree of staff division, wide extents of control, centralized authority, high degrees of specialization, and low standardization. This type of structure works best for small organizations or larger organizations with fairly simple requirements and that operate from a single location.

An example of a functional organization would be a small community newspaper owned by a national newspaper. It's run by an editor who employs six writers, who cover local news, sports, and features. The journalists communicate freely with each other about their work, but the final decision on which stories to run comes from the editor.

Divisional

Divisional organizational structures group various employees into strictly defined divisions, by location, product, or service. They often feature low specialization and narrow extents of control. This type of structure is often used by larger organizations that face diverse competition and opportunities. In such organizations, it's common to combine division structures with functional structures at lower levels.

An example of a divisional structure is a large candy manufacturer that has divisions in various cities. Each division has a president that reports to the CEO. A hierarchy of managers and employees make up each division.

Matrix

Matrix structures combine aspects of functional and divisional structures. They're typically used in highly technical organizations that depend on high levels of expertise. Matrix structures group employees using a combination of criteria, including tasks performed, product, and hierarchical rank. They may feature high staff division within departments, but low staff division over an organization or division. The extent of control can range from wide to narrow within the same organization, and high specialization may be common within departments.

An example of an organization with a matrix structure is an automotive manufacturer that relies on a high level of technical and market expertise. It requires many highly specialized functional entities but also needs the agility associated with a division structure.

Each of the types of structures has particular advantages and disadvantages. Advantages of functional structures are that they tend to encourage effective communication between individuals within departments, to improve teamwork, and to support quick decision making.

Encourage effective communication

Functional structures promote effective communication between individuals who perform similar functions. In the example of a community newspaper, there's good communication between writing staff. Often writers collaborate on stories or find ways to share out the news stories for the week.

Improve teamwork

Functional structures encourage teamwork because they group employees who perform the same or similar functions, and so generally have the same work goals. The writing staff at a community newspaper, for example, all share the goals of producing high-quality stories and meeting deadlines.

Support quick decision making

Functional structures support quick job-specific decision making because they group employees with similar, specialized expertise. In a community newspaper, for instance, all writing decisions are made efficiently as a result of a shared departmental goal, open communication, and dedicated teamwork.

Functional structures can also have disadvantages. Potentially, these include poor interdepartmental communication, and a focus on departmental rather than higher-level organizational goals.

Advantages of divisional structures are that they provide clear employee accountability, encourage hands-on problem solving, focus expertise, support delegation of responsibility, and encourage teamwork.

Provide clear accountability

In a divisional structure, employees' roles are less specialized than in a functional structure, and there's more focus on the goals of each group. This makes it easier to assess each employee's work and to reward performance appropriately.

Encourage problem solving

Divisional structures encourage hands-on problem solving because they feature low levels of specialization. Employees are able to acquire experience across varying tasks and disciplines, and learn new skills.

For example, a quality checker may be asked to fill in for an absent administrative clerk.

Focus expertise

In an organization with a divisional structure, each division typically focuses on a single product, product line, or service. This means there's a concentrated focus of expertise, and employees are encouraged to work toward highly specific product or service-related goals.

Focus on responsibility

Because a divisional structure is characterized by low specialization, managers can easily delegate tasks requiring greater responsibility to promising employees, in recognition of their hard work and diligence.

For example, a particularly hard-working administrative clerk might be delegated supervisory authority.

Encourage teamwork

Divisional structures encourage teamwork because employees in each division focus on a single product or service, and because there's low specialization. Everyone in a particular division may share tasks to achieve a required outcome.

A potential disadvantage of a divisional structure is that it can result in a lack of employees who are sufficiently specialized to train others.

This type of structure can also result in the duplication of tasks across divisions, a focus on divisional goals at the expense of overall organizational goals, and potential conflict between divisions over resources.

The matrix structure acknowledges how complex the business environment actually is. Advantages of matrix structures include better access to resources, improved technology sharing, better access to shared expertise, more democratic decision making, and more hands-on management.

Better access to resources

A matrix structure includes a wide range of divisions, potentially in many different locations. This can result in better access to resources.

An engineer working for a global automotive manufacturer, for example, might acquire specific materials for a project from a division in another city or country.

Improved technology sharing

With cooperation among multiple divisions, matrix structures offer employees improved technology sharing.

For example, an engineer spearheading a new project in one division might request research findings from a separate division working on a similar project.

Better access to shared expertise

Due to the number of highly skilled people found in matrix structures, employees have better access to shared expertise.

For example, an industrial designer working on new chassis for a car would be able to run designs past any number of highly specialized people within the organization for quick feedback.

Democratic decision making

Teams within matrix divisions often comprise highly specialized employees. These employees are usually given some authority to make democratic decisions, and this boosts morale.

Consider a team at the automotive manufacturer that's creating a new fuel filter system. When anyone encounters a problem, every person in the team has an equal opportunity to contribute to a solution.

Hands-on management

Managers in matrix organizations often share the same specialized skills as the employees they supervise, so employees experience a more hands-on style of management.

For example, a department manager heading a suspension system design project may contribute to design ideas in the same way as other department members.

A matrix structure best fits a highly technological and skill-intensive organization, such as an automobile manufacturer with numerous high-talent divisions across the globe.

A potential disadvantage of this type of structure is that it can result in employees having to report to more than one manager – for example, if a department falls under both technical and marketing superiors.

Question

Match each organizational structure to its corresponding effects on employees.

Options:

A. Functional

B. Divisional

C. Matrix

Targets:

1. Promotes good communication and teamwork, and fast decision making within teams

2. Enables fast, accurate work assessment and encourages a focus on shared goals

3. Provides easy access to resources and specialized knowledge, and supports democratic decision making and hands-on management

Answer

Functional structures group employees by task. Shared skills and a focus on the same task provide for good communication and teamwork, as well as group decision making within groups.

Divisional structures are product or service driven, so employee work and behavior can be quickly assessed and rewarded. Also, goals are shared throughout a division, and this leads to greater team spirit.

Matrix structures contain many complex functional divisions. They ensure easy access to resources, technology, and expertise. They also encourage democratic decision making and hands-on management.

Section 2 - Adapting to Organizational Structures

Section 2 - Adapting to Organizational Structures

Organizational structure affects employees' behavior in various ways, depending on employees' individual differences and levels of experience, and on the tasks they're expected to perform.

To help new employees adapt to your company's organizational structure, you can make yourself available to help, create comfort and rapport, introduce the company culture, and explain how employees' roles fit into the "bigger picture." You should also evaluate the company's structure to determine whether it's conducive to productivity, and assess any productivity problems.

How structure affects behavior

New employees can have all the necessary skills and be enthusiastic and innovative – and still be completely wrong for positions in your company. No matter how qualified they are, employees who don't fit in with the company's organizational structure won't perform well in their jobs.

Managers and HR professionals know that part of ensuring an organization's success is managing its human resources effectively. And if an organization is to have a satisfied and motivated workforce, there has to be alignment and consistency across its structure, systems, people, and culture.

So the performance of new employees depends on more than just their qualifications and previous experience. It also depends on how well the employees fit

175

in and can adapt to a company's structure and unique culture.

Organizational behavior can have dramatic effects on employees. For example, employees' performance can be negatively affected by top-heavy decisions, a lack of flexibility by managers, and unjust treatment.

Top-heavy decisions

If all key decisions in a company are made by senior managers, with little participation by other employees, it can result in low employee morale. Employees don't feel they can make a difference.

It may also be the case that managers take credit for making final decisions, while actual problem solving and the development of creative solutions occurs further down in a company. This can result in employees feeling that they're not getting the credit they deserve. If employees feel unappreciated, they're likely to lose motivation and to put less effort into their work.

Lack of flexibility

If a company is particularly inflexible about its policies and standards, and constantly checks up on work being done, employees are likely to feel mistrusted and unappreciated. This can result in the employees being less productive and producing work of lower quality.

Unjust treatment

Employees won't be loyal to an employer they feel is unjust. Also, employees who are singled out and treated unfairly may develop low self-esteem and motivation problems. They may even choose to leave the company altogether.

Certain types of organizational behavior – like unjust treatment of employees – always tend to have negative effects on employees' performance. But not all employees are the same.

The ways employees react to the elements of a company's organizational structure depend on their individual differences and experiences. This also varies based on the tasks they're expected to perform.

So it's not always easy to predict how the various elements of an organizational structure will affect employees, or what will work best. For example, a high degree of work specialization may make one employee more productive but lead to low job satisfaction for another.

The best way to ensure an employee will be a good fit for your company is to start by evaluating the company's organizational structure.

You can then identify what qualities job candidates need if they're to fit in well and be productive – and hire an employee who meets the requirements.

Most employees learn to adapt to a company's organizational structure over time. However, managers and HR professionals can smooth this process, making it faster and easier for new employees to reach their full potential. For example, simply making sure that a new employee knows what's expected or who to go to for help can save time and frustration.

Helping employees adapt

As a manager or HR professional, you can help new employees adapt to your organization's structure in various ways. You can make yourself available to new employees, create comfort and rapport, introduce the company culture, and explain the "big picture." You can also evaluate structure to determine whether it's conducive to productivity, and assess whether any productivity problems are localized or widespread.

Often a problem for a new employee is not knowing who to turn to for help or information. As a manager, you can assist by freeing up enough of your time to help and by providing the employee with your contact details. You can also arrange stand-by help for the employee, for when you're not available.

Free up time to help

As a manager, you should free up enough of your time to give a new employee needed help. For example, this might involve rescheduling meetings so you have time to show a new employee around the office and to explain how your company's intranet is set up.

A new employee who knows you're available will feel more comfortable asking questions and generally asking for help when it's needed.

Provide your contact details

You can't give up all your time to help a new employee. However, you should provide the new employee with details of how to contact you and where to find you, in case your help is needed.

Arrange stand-by help

A new employee might need help when you're in a meeting or out of the office. So it's a good idea to ask another existing employee to be on stand-by to help a new employee if you're not available. You can then tell the new employee where to find this person if you're unavailable.

Joining a new company can be a stressful experience for employees because it involves having to adapt quickly to new people and ways of doing things. You can help new employees fit in and reduce their stress by introducing them to a wide range of other employees – across different departments – and to managers, directors, and clients. Developing rapport with others is one of the best ways for new employees to relax and start settling in.

You can help a new employee meet others and establish rapport with them in several different contexts. For example, you can introduce the employee to others in a formal meeting, in casual conversations, and at break times.

You can also have a new employee spend some time with staff in each department. This will allow the employee to meet everyone in the company and get an idea of how the different departments work.

New employees will gradually accumulate knowledge about company culture – through both official information and casual conversations with other employees. But you can speed up this process, and help prevent mistakes or misunderstandings, by providing an explicit introduction to your company's culture. For example, you can give a new employee an overview of your company's management structure and communication system, and discuss various norms.

You should describe your company's culture when you first interview job candidates. This is so they know what to expect and whether your company's culture is likely to suit them. Candidates who are unlikely to be happy with your company's structure may then rule themselves out.

Once a new employee begins at your company, you can provide information about the company's culture using a formal presentation or in a guidebook. You can also consider using a buddy system, with an existing employee assigned to show a new employee how the company works.

An extra advantage of a buddy system is that it can help a new employee meet and establish rapport with colleagues. It's important to make sure that the existing employee is happy to do this, and to consider rewarding this person's efforts.

Question

Holly is about to start work as an accountant for a shipping company.

Which are examples of ways that Holly's manager, Tom, can help her adapt to the company's organizational structure?

Options:

1. Schedule time to show Holly around the company and give her his contact details

2. Take Holly to sit in on some meetings, and introduce her to other colleagues at lunch

3. Give Holly a presentation on the company's infrastructure and communication channels

4. Make sure Holly has plenty of work to keep her occupied from the outset

5. Give Holly free time to roam through the office and introduce herself to other employees

Answer

Option 1: This option is correct. To help Holly adapt, Tom should make himself available – ensuring he has the time to assist Holly and giving her his contact details so she can call on him for help if she needs it.

Option 2: This is a correct option. One of the ways Tom can make Holly more comfortable in the company is to introduce her to a wide range of employees, in formal meetings and in more casual contexts.

Option 3: This option is correct. Tom can help Holly by giving her an explicit introduction to the company's culture, including factors like its management structure and communication system.

Option 4: This is an incorrect option. Tom should focus on helping Holly adapt and fit in before giving her a heavy workload.

Option 5: This option is incorrect. It wouldn't be appropriate for Holly to wander around the offices or to disrupt other employees' work – and she may not feel confident enough to approach people she hasn't yet met. Instead Tom should introduce her to others in the company.

New employees are more likely to get up to speed quickly and to perform well if they understand how their roles fit into the bigger picture. So it's important to provide them with information about your company's history and achievements, and to explain its current goals, objectives, and focus. You could choose to do this using a slide show, for example.

It can also be useful to ask senior managers to share their insights and explain organizational goals to new employees. If a senior manager is too busy to do this, you could consider recording a video of an interview with the manager.

If new employees understand what they're working toward, and the larger context into which their roles fit, they're likely to be more motivated and productive.

As well as focusing on teaching new employees and making them feel comfortable, you should evaluate whether your company's structure is conducive to productivity. You can do this by assessing the productivity of existing employees over the long term. Short-term productivity levels are likely to be misleading – for example, because employees' productivity may decline dramatically over time. It's important to identify and address any productivity problems – and it's ideal to do this before hiring new employees.

For example, say a company implements a very flat structure, giving employees lots of freedom to manage their own time and work. It's likely that some employees will prosper in this environment, while for others it could be counterproductive.

By evaluating the company's organizational structure in this situation, you can identify the employees who need help adjusting and make changes to increase their productivity – for example, by introducing an interim supervisor.

You can also consider making changes to your company's existing structure to encourage better performance. If certain employees are struggling to be productive, for example, it might be appropriate to make slight changes to their roles – or even to completely restructure their jobs.

If you identify productivity issues during your evaluation, you should determine whether these are localized or widespread.

If the productivity problems are localized, or specific to certain employees or departments, it may be due to organizational structure. In this case, small changes – like moving employees laterally into new positions – may resolve the problems.

If productivity problems are widespread, the root causes are more likely to be systemic issues such as a lack of information flow, lack of competitive drive, or company politics.

Question Set

Noah has just been hired by an investments company. Beth, his manager, will be responsible for ensuring Noah settles in and works productively for the company.

Question 1 of 2

Which are examples of how Beth can help Noah adapt to the company's organizational structure?

Options:

1. She can reschedule a business meeting so she's free on Noah's first day and can show him around

2. She can introduce Noah to a range of people, in management meetings and informally, during breaks

3. She can evaluate current employee productivity and the need for structural changes before Noah starts work

4. She can give Noah complex and multi-layered tasks from day one so that he's forced to use his initiative

5. She can ensure that Noah has plenty of free time and space to adjust over his first three weeks

Answer

Option 1: This is a correct option. Managers can help new employees adapt by making themselves available to help. They can also assign other existing employees to help where necessary.

Option 2: This option is correct. Beth can make Noah feel more comfortable by helping him establish rapport with other employees. She can also help him become familiar with expectations and the company's cultural norms by giving him the opportunity to observe different employees' behavior in a range of contexts.

Option 3: This is a correct option. Managers like Beth should evaluate their company's organizational structure to make sure it's conducive to productivity and good employee performance. This involves examining the productivity of existing employees over the long term, and identifying any need for adjustments. It's ideal if problems are addressed before new employees are hired.

Option 4: This option is incorrect. If Noah isn't provided with any direct guidance or support, it will be difficult for him to adapt. He's likely to make mistakes and to become frustrated, and may even decide to leave the company. He may also develop inappropriate work habits that are difficult to address at a later stage.

Option 5: This is an incorrect option. Just giving a new employee free time won't help the employee learn what's required or how to fit in better with a company's organizational structure. Instead Beth should guide Noah personally, or arrange for another employee to provide him with needed help.

Question 2 of 2

In which additional ways can Beth help Noah adapt?

Options:

1. She can provide Noah with an overview of reporting structures and communication channels in the company

2. She can give Noah a booklet outlining the company's history, its current market position, and its current strategic goals

3. She can isolate and address the root causes of existing productivity problems in the company

4. She can make sure Noah knows he's free to introduce himself to everyone in the office

5. She should immediately outline the consequences of failing to meet productivity targets

Answer

Option 1: This is a correct option. Managers can help new employees adapt by providing them with a proper introduction to company culture. This includes, for example, the company's management and reporting structures, and communication channels.

185

Option 2: This option is correct. Beth can help Noah adapt by ensuring he knows how his position fits into the bigger picture of the company, including its history, current position, and strategic goals.

Option 3: This is a correct option. Managers can help ensure that new employees will perform well by identifying and addressing the causes of any existing productivity problems. This involves determining whether problems are localized or widespread, and making changes as necessary.

Option 4: This option is incorrect. It isn't appropriate to expect new employees to introduce themselves to everyone in the office. Instead Beth should make a point of introducing him to employees in different departments.

Option 5: This is an incorrect option. Although Noah should be made aware of relevant targets – preferably before he's actually hired – it's not appropriate to threaten him. If Beth starts by doing this and comes across as overly rigid, it's likely she'll simply intimidate him. This could cause Noah to lose motivation or even to leave the company.

Section 3 - Enriching Jobs Within the Organization

Section 3 - Enriching Jobs Within the Organization

Job redesign involves reallocating, or reorganizing, work responsibilities, duties, and activities. Its aim is to improve the motivation and satisfaction of employees, and so also to improve their performance and production levels.

The five primary elements of job design that affect employee behavior are skill variety, task identity, task significance, autonomy, and feedback. You can use the methods of job rotation, job enlargement, and job enrichment to redesign jobs.

The benefits of job redesign

John works in the Technical Support Department of a financial consulting organization. He has been there for seven years, his job is secure, and he's good at what he does. But there is little variety in his work, and John is really bored. In addition, he often feels unappreciated and disrespected by the company's finance professionals, whose systems he is called on to fix when things go wrong.

Put yourself in John's shoes for a moment. How would you feel knowing that every day at work is going to be the same as the day before, and that most people don't think twice about what it is that you do?

The truth is that there are many employees just like John. They feel as if their jobs and responsibilities have no real purpose.

Although it's not often possible to change the nature of a job completely, managers can use several techniques to improve the motivation and job satisfaction of employees.

One of the ways managers can sometimes improve employee performance is through job redesign. This involves reallocating, or reorganizing, the work responsibilities, duties, and activities associated with a job, to meet the needs of both the organization and the employee.

The process of job redesign has three main goals:

*   improving efficiency,
*   better matching of the individual and job tasks, and
*   improving the quality of life at work and job satisfaction.

Question

How do you think an organization can benefit from job redesign?

Options:

1. It will likely experience higher productivity
2. It will have happier and more motivated staff
3. It will have lower staff turnover
4. It will have lower training expenses
5. It can overcome all performance problems

Answer

Option 1: This is a correct option. Employees who find their jobs stimulating engage in their work with more enthusiasm, and so are more productive.

Option 2: This option is correct. Employees find well-designed jobs meaningful and stimulating. So these jobs result in better job satisfaction and motivation.

Option 3: This option is correct. Staff who are happy, secure, and fulfilled in their job situations are unlikely to look for employment options elsewhere.

Option 4: This option is incorrect. Redesigning jobs doesn't necessarily alter the skills and knowledge employees need, or the training they require.

Option 5: This is an incorrect option. Performance problems can have a wide array of root causes that don't relate to job design. For example, employees may lack required abilities or have personality clashes with their managers.

Well-designed jobs are essential for attracting and retaining a motivated work force. In most cases there are a number of alternative designs for any given job. The potential benefits for organizations that periodically redesign jobs include higher levels of productivity, a happier, more motivated workforce, and lower turnover of staff. This translates into lower costs and better business success.

Job redesign also has several potential benefits for employees:

- more interesting jobs, designed specifically to be stimulating,
- greater opportunities for promotion as a result of skills development,
- longer careers, with more potential for growth, and
- increased earning potential as a result of being assigned varied, challenging tasks.

Appropriate methods of job redesign

Various elements of job design have an effect on the behavior of employees. A popular model for understanding how particular job characteristics impact job satisfaction and other outcomes is the job characteristic model, or JCM. The characteristics it identifies as being most significant are skill variety, task identity, task significance, autonomy, and feedback.

Skill variety

Skill variety refers to the degree to which a job requires an employee to use different skills and talents. Too little variety can lead to boredom, whereas too much can be overwhelming.

For example, a mailroom clerk who sorts mail every day experiences a low level of skill variety. An administrative assistant who's responsible for typing, filing, answering telephones, and greeting clients has a much higher level of skill variety.

Task identity

Task identity refers to the extent that an employee is involved in a particular process. If employees participate in various stages of a process, they can see how their completed tasks fit in and contribute to a bigger picture. So they're likely to be more motivated than employees who form tasks in isolation, without participating in broader processes.

For example, a software engineer who writes a very specific type of code module for various projects is involved only in a very limited part of each project, and experiences a low level of task identity. Conversely, a greenhouse employee who is responsible for purchasing and planting seeds, nurturing seedlings, and selling the mature plant, is involved in the process from start to finish and experiences a high level of task identity.

Task significance

Task significance refers to the sense that a task contributes to a greater cause and benefits others. It's difficult to remain motivated if the work you do doesn't appear to make a difference – whereas knowing that something good results from your work is highly motivating and fulfilling.

For example, a doctor directly impacts patients' lives and well-being, and experiences a high level of task significance. An individual who delivers sales flyers door-to-door might experience a low level of task significance.

Autonomy

Autonomy refers to independence. Typically, employees with high degrees of independence and discretion over how they do their work are more motivated than those with little autonomy. They're responsible for the success or failure of their work, and this can be a powerful motivating factor.

For example, a teacher who decides on and plans daily learning activities has a high level of autonomy. A factory assembly-line worker who must perform repetitive tasks in accordance with strict guidelines has almost no autonomy.

Feedback

Feedback refers to the degree of response employees receive based on their efforts. It can come from a variety of sources, such as production figures, customer satisfaction scores, or a job itself. A knowledge of the outcomes of their work empowers employees to review their methods and make improvements when necessary.

For example, a software designer who builds a program and tests it gains immediate and valuable feedback about whether the program works. Another software designer who ships a product to a quality assurance manager in a different location, however, receives a lower level of feedback – which will likely be delayed and less detailed.

Question

Grant is a sales representative for a well-known pharmaceutical company.

Match each job characteristic to the example from Grant's job experience.

Options:

A. Skill variety
B. Task identity
C. Task significance
D. Autonomy
E. Feedback

Targets:

1. Grant uses a range of competencies to interpret research papers, develop presentations, and market products

2. Grant isn't sure how his efforts affect the company because he's seldom responsible for closing sales

3. Grant likes knowing that he's selling products that help sick people

4. Grant is free to decide how best to market and sell products in his portfolio

5. Grant often hears back from customers who've either liked or disliked aspects of his presentations

Answer

A job that requires the use of a wide range of competencies has a high degree of skill variety.

If it's not clear how the tasks employees perform fit into a broader process, the employees have low task identity. For example, Grant doesn't know what his efforts mean because he doesn't know their outcome.

Employees who feel their work is meaningful – for example, because it involves helping others – have high task significance.

Grant has a lot of independence over how he markets products. Another way of saying this is that he has a high degree of autonomy.

Information from customers in response to the presentations they've seen is an example of feedback. It may motivate Grant and inspire him to improve his performance.

Various factors can affect the potential for job redesign in an organization. These include the size of the organization, current and available technology, and external environment.

Size of the organization

As an organization grows and its staff, resources, and capacity expand, its structure also has to change so that its constituent parts can be coordinated.

As organizational structures become more complex, however, they often restrict flexibility. Channels of authority and procedures become more rigid, to the extent that employees may end up feeling like cogs in a machine.

Technology

The rapid development of technology and the capabilities it brings can affect the potential for job redesign. For example, the introduction of high-speed Internet connections has made it possible for many employees to work from home, while still allowing managers to monitor their work.

Technology has also increased the availability of feedback – most employees can ask for and receive feedback almost instantly using e-mail.

External environment

A range of external factors can affect the job redesign process. Some examples are new competitors entering the market, employee unions, legislation, and the current economic climate.

For instance, new workplace safety legislation may place limits on the ways jobs can be designed.

So how do you go about restructuring jobs in an organization? Three effective methods of job redesign are job rotation, job enlargement, and job enrichment.

Job rotation is the systematic shifting of employees from one job to another within an organization. It's similar to cross-training, which involves training employees how to perform a variety of roles in a process. But the goal of job rotation isn't just to equip employees to assume different roles. It's also to facilitate a more enriching work experience.

You can use job rotation when you need to staff jobs, orientate new employees, prevent job boredom, and train and develop employees for future career growth.

Job rotation can improve productivity by increasing employee interest and motivation. It can also be effective in reducing monotony, which can otherwise lead to errors in judgment and mistakes. And it can result in a more versatile workforce, reducing the impact of turnover and absenteeism.

Job enlargement involves adding tasks to a job. It's also referred to as horizontal job loading. You can use job enlargement to increase the skill range of employees, increase productivity with fewer employees, or manage employees who are experiencing burnout or have reached a plateau.

Job enrichment involves increasing an employee's level of responsibility and autonomy. It's also called vertical job loading, and represents a qualitative change in duties to increase the depth of a job.

You can use job enrichment to facilitate the development of employee competencies without the employees having to leave their current positions. Job enrichment is an effective motivational technique that allows employees to experience greater job satisfaction as a result of engaging in more meaningful tasks.

Luther, Tyrone, and Kyra have each been affected by job redesign initiatives in their respective work situations. Luther's employers have recently initiated a new system of job rotation, Tyrone has been undergoing a process of job enlargement, and Kyra's managers have been expanding her responsibilities through job enrichment.

Luther
Job rotation

Luther recently completed his degree in business administration. He wants to become a stock manager, so he applies for a position with Brocadero, a portfolio management company. The organization assigns him to a job rotation program, so his supervisor moves him from one role to the next once he has shown the necessary degree of competence.

Job rotation helps Luther achieve his career goal. He becomes a highly knowledgeable stock manager who knows everything about the production process from first-hand experience.

Tyrone
Job enlargement

Tyrone cuts the wooden casings for Phlogistics Audio's sound systems. Supervisors ask him also to cut the wooden components for their public address systems. Job enlargement allows Tyrone to extend his cutting skills to a greater variety of products. As a result, he receives more acknowledgement for his abilities.

Phlogistics Audio benefits from job enlargement because Tyrone can now do the job that was previously reserved for two.

Kyra
Job enrichment

Kyra works on the assembly line at Unito Games, a manufacturer of board and card games. Her manager wants to make her job less monotonous, so he asks her if she'd be interested in learning how to supervise the delivery of stock to her section of the factory. She agrees. The added responsibility encourages Kyra to become a more active member of the production team, and helps her expand her skills.

The organization benefits because when the stock controller for Kyra's section is on leave, she's able to take over his duties.

Like all processes of change, job redesign isn't always well received. It can also be complicated because an organization needs to maintain productivity while new jobs are developed. Good preparation is the key to success. Some helpful guidelines for engaging in effective job redesign are to set clear objectives and timelines, ensure stakeholder agreement, involve staff, and manage and monitor change.

Set clear objectives and timelines

You need to be clear about the redesign project's objectives from the outset. These objectives describe the plan's outcomes and serve as the guide for the redesign process. An example of a clear objective could be to improve productivity, to increase job satisfaction, or to improve staff retention.

You also need to establish realistic timelines, taking factors such as peak business periods and vacation times into consideration.

Ensure stakeholder agreement

It's essential that you gain the support of key stakeholders within the organization. This is because job redesign usually has an impact on multiple departments and functional areas.

Key stakeholders can include managers and leaders, representatives of employee unions, and the HR and IT Departments.

Involve staff members

You should strive to include the affected employees in the job redesign process, right from the outset. These employees have practical experience of the relevant jobs and so can contribute valuable insights. Involving affected staff also makes it more likely they'll be open to the changes associated with redesigned jobs.

Manage and monitor changes

It's important that you're proactive in managing and monitoring change. This involves preparing staff for the impending changes by communicating their benefits and providing the necessary training, and evaluating the situation post-implementation to ensure that everything is progressing as it should.

Case Study: Question 1 of 2

Scenario

Margaret is a customer relations consultant at a company that sells locally produced music online. She is known as a hard worker and her manager, Gabriel, has never had reason to be concerned about her performance before. Her efficiency in the office has always been a good reflection on him as a manager. Margaret's responsibilities include writing e-mail newsletters to current and potential customers regarding new albums and artists, and responding to complaints and queries.

Gabriel has started to notice that Margaret is losing interest in her work. Increasing numbers of customers are complaining about delays in her responses to their queries, and fewer newsletters are being sent out each month. Gabriel would love to find a way to help Margaret find a renewed sense of enjoyment and satisfaction in her work.

Answer the questions in the given order.

Question

Which issues make it appropriate to redesign Margaret's job?

Options:

1. Gabriel is concerned that Margaret's declining performance will reflect negatively on his abilities as a manager

2. As a manager, Gabriel is solely responsible for ensuring that Margaret enjoys her job

3. Margaret performs an important functional role but experiences little in the way of skill variety or task identity

4. Margaret has already proved that she can handle her current responsibilities, and is probably bored

Answer

Option 1: This is an incorrect answer. Although Gabriel might legitimately be concerned about his own performance as a manager, job redesign is concerned with finding the balance between Margaret's needs and the organization's needs.

Option 2: This answer is incorrect. As a manager, Gabriel should try to ensure that his employees are happy and productive. However, Margaret also needs to take responsibility and to work with Gabriel to find a workable solution.

Option 3: This option is correct. Margaret may be more motivated and productive if she's able to use a wider variety of skills in her job, and to participate in a broader process so she knows what difference her work makes.

Option 4: This is a correct option. Margaret is becoming increasingly unhappy in her job and this is affecting her performance. A fresh challenge in the form of new job responsibilities may renew her motivation and sense of purpose.

Case Study: Question 2 of 2

Which method of job redesign is most appropriate in Margaret's situation?

Options:

1. Give her more tasks to do, to keep her busy. Gabriel has her improve the newsletter by splitting it into four separate newsletters that are specialized by musical genre and sent out according to customers' musical tastes and purchasing history.

2. Give her the responsibility of creating, managing, and maintaining an interactive blog for the company's web site. On the site, she'll be able to review new bands and albums, and interact with the comments and opinions posted by users of the site.

3. Give her the responsibility of planning and running a departmental course on improved customer communication, entitled "How to talk to the customer who is always right."

Answer

Option 1: This option is incorrect. Giving Margaret more tasks would enlarge her job – but in this case, she'd still doing the same things and using the same skills every day. She'd just be under greater pressure because of a heavier workload.

Option 2: This option is correct. Gabriel should recognize Margaret's need for more variety in her job. Giving her responsibility for creating and managing an interactive blog for the company will draw on skills and talents she isn't currently using. It's likely to give Margaret a renewed sense of excitement about her job – and to benefit the company by increasing its level of interaction with potential customers.

Option 3: This option is incorrect. Although a new responsibility in a new skill field like facilitation will certainly be important for her personal development, she's unlikely to be excited about the content of the course, seeing as customers haven't been entirely satisfied with her service recently. So this solution doesn't address any of the root problems that are affecting her current work performance.

CHAPTER 5 -a Positive Organizational Culture

CHAPTER 5 -a Positive Organizational Culture

Section 1 - What is a Positive Workplace Culture?

Section 1 - What is a Positive Workplace Culture?

A positive workplace culture has benefits for organizations and their employees. It provides employees with stability and a sense of identity, and maximizes employee engagement and productivity.

Characteristics of a positive workplace culture include trust, fairness, and respect; open, honest communication; recognition and rewards for employees' efforts; focus on teamwork; opportunities for learning, training and development; and encouragement of a healthy work-life balance.

Benefits of a positive culture

Can a company thrive in the business world regardless of how employees feel about working there? The answer is probably no. A positive workplace culture is key to an organization's success.

Every morning, Angela and her colleagues greet each other with a friendly smile.

When Angela has a problem with some aspect of her work, she knows she can approach her manager who is always quick to help or refer her to someone who can help.

And whenever the team must meet a deadline or overcome a problem, everyone – including Angela's manager – helps out and works together.

The attitudes and behavior of employees are usually a reflection of the culture of an organization. Every company has a unique organizational culture – a way of doing and interpreting things that influences how its employees view themselves, each other, and their work.

Angela's company, for example, has a positive organizational culture. Employees in the company are happy and, in turn, highly productive. As a result, the company is well equipped to satisfy its customers and meet its business goals.

In an organization with a negative culture, the ways employees feel and behave can prevent the organization from succeeding. For example, employees who feel unfairly treated and lack motivation may provide very poor customer service – resulting in losses for their company.

Question

Do you think everyone in a company typically has the same organizational culture?

Options:

1. Yes
2. No

Answer

Option 1: This option is incorrect. Actually, different groups – like employees in different departments – may have different cultures within the same organization.

Option 2: This is the correct option. An organization may have subcultures, or different cultures that characterize different groups of employees. In an advertising agency, for example, people in the Design Department might have a much more informal culture – with more emphasis on being creative – than people in the Finance Department.

An organization's culture, and any subcultures it includes, evolves gradually. Each person involved in the organization has a unique set of experiences, perceptions, and values, and these help shape the organization's culture. As an organization grows and hires new personnel, aspects of its culture usually become more entrenched and may be put into writing. However, the organization's culture continues to be influenced by those who join it.

An organization's culture is also influenced by other factors:

- prevailing societal norms in the region where the organization is located,
- the need to respond to specific external challenges such as a harsh economic climate, and
- the structure of the organization – for example, a company where only top-level managers are authorized to make decisions will generally have a fairly rigid, hierarchical culture.

Question

What do you think are the benefits of a positive workplace culture?

Options:

1. It provides employees with stability
2. It raises corporate share value
3. It instills a sense of identity and belonging
4. It eliminates the need to manage employees' performance
5. It maximizes employee engagement
6. It maximizes productivity

Answer

Option 1: This is a correct option. A positive workplace culture gives employees a sense of belonging and stability, and so results in lower turnover.

Option 2: This is an incorrect option. A company's culture influences how well it runs but doesn't directly affect the value of its shares.

Option 3: This is a correct option. In an organization with a positive culture, employees work well together, like their jobs and where they work, and view their roles as contributing to organizational success. In turn, they experience a sense of identity and belonging.

Option 4: This is an incorrect option. Although a positive workplace can make employees want to take on more responsibilities, it doesn't eliminate the need for effective performance management.

Option 5: This is a correct option. Employees who view themselves as assets to their organization tend to be more productive and loyal, and more engaged in their work.

Option 6: This is a correct option. Employees who like their work and work environment are more motivated and more productive than those who don't.

So the benefits of a positive workplace culture are significant. This type of culture gives employees a sense of stability, and a sense of identity and belonging. It also results in more engaged employees and higher productivity.

Characteristics of a positive culture

A positive workplace culture promotes employee job satisfaction and loyalty, and results in better performance. It can mean the difference between success and failure for an organization.

However, a positive workplace culture isn't built overnight. It's carefully developed through a series of initiatives at all levels of an organization, and relies on everyone having the same vision.

The culture must be maintained and fostered through the efforts of all employees and through effective leadership.

No two organizations are completely alike – and their cultures aren't either. But what makes for a positive workplace culture? Consider two companies – Sonical Electronics and Zoflina – with widely different cultures, but whose cultures contribute significantly to their success.

Sonical Electronics

At Sonical Electronics, employees know that when problems occur or they make mistakes, they can inform their supervisors, and they won't be blamed for issues outside their control.

Employees treasure the value of working together. Good team and individual performances are rewarded with production bonuses.

An ongoing management training program is just one of the professional development programs available to interested employees. The company also has its own in-house gym, which employees are free to use during their breaks and before or after work.

Zoflina

Fashion designers at Zoflina are encouraged to be creative. Regular feedback sessions with a head designer mean they often have their work appraised and the discussions are frank.

Designers often have different opinions but they work well together, with everyone brainstorming different ideas to develop the best possible designs.

Zoflina has its own "Creative Flair of the Month" team award. It subsidizes further study on industry-related courses on a review basis. It also insists that employees use their full allowances of vacation time each year.

As a manager or human resources professional, it's not enough only to react to individual personnel issues when they arise. You also need to have a good understanding of the characteristics of a positive workplace culture so you can begin shaping one from the outset. Both Sonical Electronics and Zoflina, for example, have cultures marked by these characteristics.

A positive workplace culture has six main characteristics:

- people treat one another with trust, fairness, and respect,
- there's an open forum for honest communication,
- employees receive recognition and rewards for good performance,
- teamwork and participation marks the culture,
- employees are provided with learning, training, and development opportunities, and
- employees are encouraged to maintain a good work-life balance.

Trust and communication

Trust, fairness, and respect are essential whenever a group of people need to work toward a common goal. Without these attributes, it can be difficult and demoralizing for employees to work together.

Angela's manager and her colleagues at Portage Airlines are always polite and listen carefully to what she has to say.

They trust that they won't be given unreasonable tasks and that their efforts will be recognized.

Also, they believe that their fellow employees and managers will consider their best interests as well as the interests of the organization when making decisions. For example, when Angela needs to meet a deadline but one of her children falls seriously ill, her manager and colleagues help her meet that deadline while she takes time off to care for her child.

Trust, fairness, and respect in the workplace help ensure harmonious interactions. Employees are more likely to feel that they're valued and the system is inherently fair.

And employees typically reciprocate – if they're treated fairly and with respect, they're likely to go out of their way to help their organization succeed.

Question

Which example demonstrates trust, fairness, and respect in the workplace?

Options:

1. A manager allows team members to leave work a couple of hours early after they put in overtime to meet a deadline

2. A manager allows an employee to go home early because the employee seems bored

3. A manager demands that employees start putting in overtime because the company is struggling

Answer

Option 1: This is the correct option. The employees trust that the system is fair, and therefore go out of their way to meet a deadline. The manager then reciprocates by allowing them to go home early, which helps develop mutual respect.

Option 2: This is an incorrect option. Allowing an apparently bored employee to go home early isn't fair to other employees.

Option 3: This option is incorrect. Demanding that employees put in overtime won't make them feel positive about working for the company. It also won't win the employees' respect.

Open, honest communication is always a feature of a positive workplace culture. It's the basis for successful cooperation. An open channel of communication between managers and employees fosters trust and understanding, and makes employees feel included in company processes. Employees arealso more willing to make concessions or adapt to changes if there's open communication.

Say managers of a call center decide to start clamping down on employees who arrive late for work. Without warning, they subject latecomers to disciplinary action.

Several employees, including some of the company's best performers, are taken by surprise when they're disciplined for arriving just minutes late. They become resentful and simply less willing to put in extra effort for the company.

In an organization with a more positive culture, managers would typically have a meeting to inform employees about any changes in policy that could affect them, provide background information about these changes, and invite their feedback.

At Portage Airlines, the CEO decides that no bonuses will be awarded until the company has survived a difficult financial period. He sends an e-mail to all members of staff, clearly explaining why this is necessary and asking for their understanding.

The members of staff overcome their initial disappointment because the decision was properly explained. So in this case, open communication helped ensure employees' willingness to support the company through a difficult period.

Question

A company wants to increase production, so it records employees' output and presents a table of their scores to them without warning. The table shows where improvements need to be made.

Do you think this is an example of open, honest communication?

Options:

1. Yes

2. No

Answer

Company managers should have informed employees about the new scoring system, explained their reasons for implementing it, and allowed employees to voice any concerns. Instead, they imposed a decision unilaterally and without communicating about it. Employees may respond negatively as a result.

Recognition and teamwork

Recognition and employee rewards are important motivators. People need to feel appreciated for their efforts and to know they'll be fairly rewarded if they perform well. And when they are recognized for their efforts, it can make them want to do even better in the future.

Erika is an employee who has been with Portage Airlines for nearly three years. Recently, she received a surprise in her inbox – a note of congratulation for the excellent work she'd done over the past week. Everybody was copied with the e-mail, which made Erika feel very proud. It affirmed her and made other employees want to achieve similar successes.

Teamwork is a hallmark of a positive working culture. Ideally, all employees feel that their efforts contribute directly to the success of their company and are enthusiastic about participating in a collective effort. They readily support one another, and there's no malicious competitiveness.

Consider Portage Airlines and one of its competitors, Yourway Airline, and how teamwork features in both of them.

Portage Airlines

At Portage Airlines, employees help each other out, whether in the ticket office or at the baggage counter, and strive to provide good customer service. Different functions are interdependent and each staff member relies on the next to facilitate work flow. Employees know that their roles are important and often exceed their own job descriptions to support the efforts of others.

Yourway Airline

Yourway Airline is a company that values individual achievements over team performance. Employees are fiercely competitive, often comparing themselves to their colleagues to make sure they aren't being outdone. Employees who achieve the highest sales are awarded large bonuses. No reward is given for working together to fix problems or for providing excellent customer service.

Portage Airlines has better success than its competitor because of its understanding of the concept of teamwork. Employees at Yourway Airline are less successful at keeping customers happy and loyal because they're rewarded only for their individual sales scores. The employees at Portage Airlines, on the other hand, work together to overcome problems and provide excellent service, contributing to their company's success.

Development and balance

Learning, training, and development opportunities are another characteristic of a positive workplace culture. This is because work without any prospects of advancement can eventually become tedious or seem meaningless. Giving employees opportunities to grow and to advance their careers can keep them motivated and satisfied in their jobs.

Gabriel has been working in the sales office at Portage Airlines for many years. He has always wanted to play a more influential role in the day-to-day running of the business.

Recently, Gabriel decided to take advantage of a management training course Portage Airlines offers to exceptional employees. He's very motivated and hopes to become a regional sales manager.

Question

What do you think are the likely consequences of Gabriel receiving training?

Options:

1. He'll have new or improved skills to contribute to the company

2. He'll soon be tempted to take his new skills to another company

3. He's likely to feel more motivated and to strive to perform at his best

4. He'll get a promotion

Answer

Option 1: This is a correct option. Training is likely to add to or improve the skills that Gabriel brings to the company.

Option 2: This is an incorrect option. It's likely that Gabriel will be more loyal to his company because of the faith it has shown in him by giving him management training. This makes it less likely that he'll leave to work for a competitor.

Option 3: This option is correct. By meeting Gabriel's need for challenges and progress in his career, the company helps motivate him to perform at his best.

Option 4: This is an incorrect option. Gabriel is more likely to be promoted because of the additional training, but it's not guaranteed that he'll be promoted. It may take additional training and more work experience to achieve a promotion.

Good work-life balance is a final, important characteristic of a positive workplace culture. Employees work better if they're less stressed. They're also likely to be loyal to a company that respects their needs outside of work – including those related to family life, physical health, and emotional well-being.

Management can help employees achieve a good work-life balance through policies and practices such as flextime, vacations – which may even be mandatory – and family-based benefits, including parental leave.

Some companies also have onsite facilities – like their own gyms or recreation rooms – where employees can relax when they're not working.

Betty works for Portage Airlines at ticket sales. She has three children in school, and the company lets her work part of her lunch break and then leave work early each day to pick them up.

Every morning, she works out at the small gym the company provides for employees. She says it gives her energy for the rest of the day.

Portage Airlines also has a pleasant cafeteria where employees can relax and even watch TV during their lunch breaks.

Management at Portage Airlines helps ensure Betty's workplace culture is a positive one by helping employees balance the work they do with meeting family obligations, exercising, and relaxing.

Question Set

A positive workplace culture has specific characteristics.

Question 1 of 2

Question

Which are examples of the characteristics of a positive workplace culture?

Options:

1. A company changes its recruitment policy and all employees receive an e-mail explaining why

2. Team members avoid sharing information and compete to see who can be most productive

3. Employees don't want to ask for further training in case this makes them seem unsatisfied with their current jobs

4. Employers bring outstanding achievements by particular employees to the attention of the rest of the company

5. Managers ensure workloads are reasonable and evenly distributed, and always take employees' needs into consideration

Answer

Option 1: This is a correct option. In a positive workplace culture, managers and employees communicate openly and honestly. For example, managers clearly explain any changes that may affect employees.

Option 2: This is an incorrect option. Sometimes competition is healthy, and at other times it can be destructive. It isn't a characteristic of a positive workplace culture, in which team members work well together to achieve shared objectives.

Option 3: This is an incorrect option. A characteristic of a positive workplace culture is support for employee training and development. If employees don't have opportunities to develop their skills and advance in their careers, they're likely to lose motivation and become less productive over time.

Option 4: This option is correct. A characteristic of a positive workplace culture is that employees are recognized and fairly rewarded for their efforts.

Option 5: This is a correct option. Trust, respect, and fairness are essential characteristics of a positive workplace culture. Managers may build a positive culture by, for example, ensuring work is fairly distributed and respecting employees' needs.

Question 2 of 2

Which are additional examples of the characteristics of a positive workplace culture?

Options:

1. Employees who want to find out about new company policies must write to the CEO

2. Employees who feel their job roles permit no opportunity for advancement can train further

3. A company has its own gym for employees to use during their breaks

4. Members of a team support one another and share their skills to achieve common goals

5. A manager often takes credit for the work of the employees she supervises

Answer

Option 1: This is an incorrect option. Employers in a positive workplace environment communicate openly through e-mails or meetings with employees about policy shifts.

Option 2: This is a correct option. A company with a positive workplace culture provides employees with opportunities for learning and development.

Option 3: This is a correct option. A positive workplace culture depends on employees achieving a good work-life balance. Providing a gym so that employees can fit exercise into their work days is one example of how to do this.

Option 4: This is a correct option. A characteristic of a positive workplace culture is good teamwork, with team members who support one another and work well together to achieve shared goals.

Option 5: This is an incorrect option. A positive workplace culture depends on trust and fairness. Employees are likely to lose motivation and become resentful if a manager takes unfair credit for their work.

Section 2 - Drivers of Organizational Culture

Section 2 - Drivers of Organizational Culture

Organizational culture serves several functions, including reminding employees of their organizations' goals, encouraging social stability, and providing employees with a sense of belonging. Employees affect organizational culture. In addition, their behavior, job satisfaction, and productivity are affected by organizational culture.

Amiability, job autonomy, and degree of structure drive organizational culture. Recognition and rewards also play a role, as do opportunities for professional growth. Other factors driving organizational culture are tolerance for risk and change, response to concerns, and diversity.

Amiability and job autonomy

Organizational culture can be described as the collective personality of an organization. The employees in the organization contribute to and influence its culture by bringing their own personalities, experiences, preferences, and perceptions to the working environment.

However, the relationship also goes the other way. Organizational culture affects employees' behavior, as well as their job satisfaction and productivity.

This makes organizational culture very important, because it impacts the organization's ability to fulfill its mission and vision.

An organizational culture has several functions. It reminds employees of the organization's goals, encourages social stability, and provides employees with a sense of belonging. It also facilitates informal communication.

Question

Which statements about organizational culture are true?

Options:

1. It affects the behavior of employees in an organization

2. It doesn't influence an organization's ability to fulfill its mission

3. It's affected by the employees within an organization

4. It's determined solely by the approach of an organization's management

Answer

Option 1: This option is correct. Organizational culture affects employees' job satisfaction and productivity.

Option 2: This is an incorrect option. One of the functions of organizational culture is to remind employees of the organization's goals, which play a part in its mission.

Option 3: This is a correct option. Employees contribute to organizational culture by bringing their own personalities, experiences, preferences, and perceptions to the working environment.

Option 4: This option is incorrect. Both managers and other employees in an organization affect organizational culture.

Eight main factors, or drivers, affect organizational culture:

- amiability in the work environment,
- job autonomy given to employees,
- degree of structure in the organization,
- recognition and rewards given to employees,
- opportunities for professional growth afforded to employees,

- tolerance for risk and change by organizational members,
- management response to concerns, and
- diversity of the workforce.

Amiability refers to warmth and friendliness, or approachability.

An organization with a "family" atmosphere, for example, is much more amiable than one where the atmosphere is cold and impersonal.

You can gauge an organization's amiability by observing how friendly people are in their social interactions – in both formal and informal environments – and how much they socialize. For example, do employees socialize with one another during their breaks? Or, when it's someone's birthday, does the organization hold some sort of celebration?

In any organization, employees are given varying levels of autonomy. This refers to their freedom to do their work independently, without having to consult colleagues or management about exactly how to do it. Some organizations give their employees more autonomy than others.

Employees' levels of autonomy depend partly on the types of work they do. For example, a highly qualified researcher will typically work more independently than someone on a construction team.

But management also plays a role by deciding how much autonomy to give employees.

For example, a project manager may assign the marketing manager and the team members with either a low or high level of autonomy.

Low autonomy

With low autonomy, the marketing manager must consult the project manager when drawing up the marketing plan. The project manager also has to approve all marketing-related decisions before they're implemented. For example, the marketing manager has to gain authorization before taking steps like issuing press releases, or printing posters and flyers.

High autonomy

With high autonomy, the project manager gives the marketing manager permission to plan and execute the entire marketing plan. The marketing manager takes total responsibility for this plan and doesn't have to run decisions by the project manager.

Structure, recognition, and rewards

Another driver of organizational culture is the degree of structure in an organization. This depends on how rigidly employee behavior is regulated through official policies, procedures, and guidelines. For example, two companies – Earth Farm and Diallonics – have very different degrees of structure, and this is reflected in their cultures.

Earth Farm

Earth Farm, a home business with a small staff complement, has a low degree of structure, with very few documented policies or rules.

Employees find out how things must be done as they work or by speaking to the owner or other employees.

Diallonics

Diallonics, a multinational corporation, has a high degree of structure, with documented information about everything from dress code to disciplinary procedures and the policy for overtime pay.

New employees are given access to this information in printed documents, such as rule books, or on the company's intranet.

Organizational culture is also driven by the level of recognition and reward given to employees. Employees are likely to be more motivated and productive if managers acknowledge good performance and show appreciation for their efforts. Rewards can also serve as incentives to work hard or meet particular targets.

Methods of recognition and reward include monetary rewards, such as cash bonuses, salary increases, or even gift vouchers. They can also include nonmonetary rewards, like giving employees time off, promotions, certificates or awards, or the freedom to choose work assignments.

From a management perspective, some organizations recognize and reward employees to a greater extent than others. On the employee side, expectations about rewards also differ.

The extent to which each side focuses on recognition and reward influences the organizational culture.

Question

Easy Nomad Travel employs 25 travel agents who are tasked with getting customers the best value for money in quality leisure resorts and locations.

Which statements describe how structure, recognition, and rewards drive the organizational culture at the company?

Options:

1. Agents are careful about the way they work because they have to handle bookings according to the company's documented operating procedures

2. Agents are friendly and good-spirited, often having informal birthday parties for each other in the office

3. Agents work hard to sell more than 15 travel packages each month, as this target earns them a 10% salary bonus for the month

4. Senior agents enjoy freedom in their work because they can negotiate special prices for loyal customers, within certain predefined limits

Answer

Option 1: This option is correct. Documented procedures give an element of structure to the organizational culture, with agents cautiously adhering to company expectations.

Option 2: This is an incorrect option. This behavior is not related to structure, recognition, or rewards. It relates to amiability in the work environment.

Option 3: This is a correct option. Monetary rewards add motivation to the organizational culture, with agents striving to beat a monthly target so they can earn a bonus.

Option 4: This option is incorrect. This behavior isn't related to structure, recognition, or rewards. It relates to job autonomy in the work environment.

Growth, risk, and change

Opportunities for professional growth act as another driver of organizational culture. Both organizations and employees can benefit when employees improve their knowledge and skills. And when organizations encourage such advancement, this progressiveness has a positive effect on the organizational culture.

Organizations can give their employees various types of development opportunities:

- sending employees for management courses,
- having employees attend training seminars, both inside and outside the organization,
- subsidizing employees' university or college studies, and
- acquiring new books or e-learning courses.

An organizational culture is also driven by people's openness to taking risks and making changes.

In this sphere, you need to look at how willing the organization is to be creative and innovative, and how easily it adopts new ideas and makes adjustments to adapt to the changing business environment.

Based on their levels of risk tolerance and openness to change, you can generally categorize organizations as highly traditional, moderate, or highly innovative. For example, take three companies: Bleewell Insurance, Sonical Electronics, and Award Sportswear.

Bleewell Insurance

Bleewell Insurance is highly traditional, putting heavy emphasis on stability. It encourages its employees to work according to standard company methods and to do things the way they've always been done, so that the company maintains its solid reputation of reliability.

Sonical Electronics

As a consumer goods company that needs to be aware of its competition, Sonical Electronics encourages planned risk and change – striking a balance between the traditional and very innovative mind sets. It encourages employees to remain stable but also be creative and open to change if those changes have been well considered.

Award Sportswear

Award Sportswear aims to revolutionize the sports apparel industry and is therefore highly innovative. It is very open to change, showing a willingness to make big innovations and take risks in the hope that this strategy will be profitable and help it change the industry. The company encourages its employees to use their creativity to come up with unconventional plans that competitors may not have tried.

Concerns and diversity

The way an organization responds to its employees' concerns is another factor driving organizational culture. Organizations differ in their sensitivity to the issues and problems employees encounter, and this helps shape employees' perception of how much they're valued.

You can ask several questions to get a measure of how responsive an organization is to particular employee concerns:

*   How quickly does the organization respond to the employees' concerns?
*   Is the response satisfactory to the employees?
*   Is the response genuine?
*   Is the response effective in resolving the concern?

Question

Adam, a new employee, is having a problem with the air conditioning in his office. The air flow aggravates his sinuses, which give him severe headaches. As a result, he's struggling to do his work. He brings the problem to the attention of his team leader, Joan.

Which response shows the highest level of organizational concern for Adam's problem?

Options:

1. Joan promises to take the issue up with the company manager at the next team leader meeting in two weeks' time

2. Joan offers Adam a painkiller and tells him to stop complaining about minor issues

3. Joan sympathizes and immediately gives Adam the option to move to a desk where the air flow won't affect him as badly

Answer

Option 1: This is an incorrect option. Although this response is genuine and could be effective, it's not timely and doesn't satisfy Adam, who needs the problem addressed urgently.

Option 2: This option is incorrect. Although this response is timely and could be an effective short-term solution, it's insensitive and doesn't satisfy Adam, who needs a long-term solution.

Option 3: This is the correct option. This response shows the most concern because it's quick, effective, genuine, and likely to be satisfactory to Adam.

A final driver of organizational culture is diversity. Diversity includes ethnicity, but also extends to other characteristics like gender, age, religion, level of training, status in the workplace, and even family situation – such as marital status and number of children. Organizations vary in how diverse their workforces are.

Because society is diverse, it's important to have a diverse workforce that includes a spectrum of different types of people.

This can make your workforce more adaptable to the needs of an ever-changing customer market. The diverse people in the organization can give you valuable, varied perspectives that contribute to better solutions.

Diversity also gives an organization a broader range of skills and experience to draw on. So it can increase productivity, creativity, and quality of work.

For example, a marketing team that consists of diverse employees is well placed to come up with promotional techniques that appeal to various market segments.

In addition to the main factors that drive organizational culture, several other factors have some influence on culture. These include management definition, physical environment, social structure, industry or professional culture, and branding.

Management definition

Management may attempt to define or dictate organizational culture. This could influence the culture, but isn't a driver of the culture.

Organizational culture is the reality that is lived in the organization – not necessarily what is claimed by management. The culture is defined, driven, and shared collaboratively by all the members of the organization.

Physical environment

The type of physical environment the organization operates in may influence its organizational culture. For example, in a city center office block, the culture might be more fast-paced and characteristic of urban living – as opposed to the more laid back atmosphere and culture of a company with offices in a remote rural or suburban location.

However, the employees and interactions within that physical environment set the actual organizational culture. It's not defined by the environment itself.

Social structure

An organization's social structure could influence its organizational culture, although the two concepts aren't the same.

The social structure deals with the relationships and interactions between organizational members. Organizational culture relates to the behavioral patterns, values, and assumptions that arise from those interactions.

Industry or professional culture

Computer programmers may tend to use technical terms, and sales professionals may tend to exaggerate the benefits of their products. These shared characteristics are part of industry or professional cultures; employees share them because of the type of work they do.

These characteristics influence – but aren't the same as – organizational culture, which is a set of behavioral patterns, values, and assumptions specific to a particular organization.

Branding

An organization's branding may influence its culture, but branding isn't the actual culture itself. Catchphrases, logos, and other symbols are merely representations of organizational culture.

Question Set

A variety of factors influence and shape organizational culture.

Question 1 of 2

Question

Brocadero Pharmaceuticals is a leading pharmaceutical manufacturer, focusing on efficiency and excellence in product development. What are the drivers of organizational culture in this scenario?

Options:

1. Brocadero's social scene is characterized by professionally-based cliques

2. Brocadero moves quickly to resolve issues affecting employee productivity

3. Brocadero lets employees work independently

4. Brocadero operates from an industrial suburb outside a major city

5. Brocadero prefers to employ only certain types of people

6. Brocadero discourages socializing that isn't related to work

Answer

Option 1: This is an incorrect option. Social structure can influence organizational culture, but it's not an actual driver of organizational culture.

Option 2: This option is correct. Brocadero's quick response to employee concerns is shown in its prompt action when employees' productivity is threatened.

Option 3: This is a correct option. Brocadero's high degree of job autonomy is reflected in the high level of independence it grants to employees.

Option 4: This option is incorrect. Physical environment may influence organizational culture, but it's not a driver of organizational culture.

Option 5: This option is correct. Brocadero's low level of diversity is shown in its narrowly focused recruitment policies, which favor elite college graduates and middle- to upper-class income earners.

Option 6: This is a correct option. Brocadero's low amiability is shown in its strong emphasis on work efficiency, with no social events and limited social interaction.

Question 2 of 2

Unito Properties is a new real estate agency, managed by its owner and employing a staff complement of 20 people.

Access the learning aid Unito Properties Scenario to help you answer this question.

What are the drivers of organizational culture in this scenario?

Options:

1. Unito invests in its employees by encouraging them to improve their skills and knowledge

2. Unito operates without detailed policies and procedures

3. Unito's experienced agents give the younger agents tips on how to succeed in the real estate business

4. Unito operates in a professional, efficient, customer-focused manner

5. Unito allows employees to use their creativity to achieve business success 6. Unito offers financial incentives to employees who excel in their work

Answer

Option 1: This is a correct option. Unito encourages its employees' professional growth by sending them to courses and conferences.

Option 2: This option is correct. Unito's low level of structure is evident in its lack of official documentation.

Option 3: This is an incorrect option. Aspects of the real estate agents' professional culture can influence organizational culture, but they don't drive organizational culture.

Option 4: This option is incorrect. Unito's informal and sometimes disorganized method of operation doesn't reflect the organizational culture that the owner would like the company to have.

Option 5: This option is correct. Unito's high tolerance for risk and change is shown in its encouragement of innovative advertising methods.

Option 6: This is a correct option. Unito's high level of recognition and appreciation is shown in the rewards it gives to outstanding performers. These include cash, time off, and stock options.

Section 3 - Strategies for Cultivating a Positive Culture

Section 3 - Strategies for Cultivating a Positive Culture

A positive culture in the workplace results in happier employees, higher productivity, lower turnover, and better customer satisfaction. However, it's not easy to change an organization's culture. This requires an all-encompassing approach that focuses on every aspect of an organization and that includes all its members.

Strategies you can use to promote a positive organizational culture include influencing employees through leadership, developing a sense of belonging and a sense of history among employees, focusing on employee satisfaction, and fostering diversity.

Promoting a positive culture

It's important to cultivate and maintain a positive workplace culture for several reasons. It is more likely that a large proportion of employees are happy and motivated, which translates into higher productivity. They're more likely to want to stay with their organization, resulting in lower turnover. Also, happier employees provide better customer service. So a positive culture helps generate improved customer satisfaction.

An organization's culture can be hard to define, and difficult to manage and change.

This doesn't mean that you can't alter an organization's culture to make it more positive. But doing this requires an all-encompassing and directive approach that includes everyone in the organization. Focusing on just one aspect of culture – like diversity or the degree of independence employees have in their work – won't be enough.

You can help cultivate a positive workplace culture using several strategies. You can use your influence through leadership, develop a sense of belonging and oneness, develop a sense of history, focus on employee satisfaction, and foster diversity.

Leadership, belonging, and history

The leadership in an organization has a significant effect on how productive and loyal employees are. It also affects how positive they feel about their work. So as a leader, you're in a position to influence employees in ways that lead to a more positive culture. To do this, you need to make employees want to follow you. You also need to demonstrate qualities such as integrity and provide clear direction and focus.

Make employees want to follow

You might be able to make employees work just by telling them what to do and exerting the formal power you have as a manager. But this won't help you change the way employees think and feel.

If you want employees to view their jobs and their organization in a more positive light, you have to become someone they want to follow. You need to inspire employees with the vision and optimism you portray, and encourage everyone to participate in making the organization a success. You also need to ensure every employee feels like a valued member of the organization.

Demonstrate integrity

Before you can influence employees, you have to be the kind of leader they feel they can admire. So it's vital that you demonstrate qualities such as honesty, authenticity, and integrity.

Over time, this will help you earn employees' trust and respect. It's also likely to encourage employees to demonstrate similar qualities in return. And employees who have faith in an organization's leaders generally feel more positive about the organization and their contributions to it.

Provide clear direction

A leader should provide clear direction and focus so that all employees understand exactly what they're working toward. This involves ensuring employees are familiar with the organization's vision and objectives, and understand how their roles support these.

Without this type of direction, employees may fail to understand how their efforts make a difference or what their purpose is. This situation can lead to poor motivation.

Conversely, having shared goals unites and inspires employees, making them more positive about their work.

The manager of a sales team in a company that assembles and sells computers is concerned about the team's comparatively low sales.

She notices that team members often arrive at work late. Team spirit is low and team members seldom laugh or even talk to one another. In interviews, some team members admit to being bored and uninspired.

Question

Which are effective ways for the team manager to use her leadership position to cultivate a more positive workplace culture?

Options:

1. Crack down on team members, explaining that if their sales don't improve, they may face disciplinary action

2. In a team meeting, discuss the company's vision of becoming the leading retailer of computers and explain exactly how the sales team can help in achieving this

3. Give each team member a more challenging sales target for the coming quarter

4. Communicate excitement about the team's goals and about individual team members' achievements on a daily basis

5. Always treat team members fairly and accept blame from senior managers when problems are her fault

Answer

Option 1: This is an incorrect option. The manager might succeed in getting the team to perform better – at least over the short term – by threatening team members with negative consequences for poor performance. However, this won't do anything to improve the team members' attitudes or levels of motivation. It won't contribute to a more positive organizational culture and is unlikely to improve performance over the long term.

Option 2: This option is correct. The manager can help cultivate a more positive culture by giving the team members direction and focus. One way of doing this is to make it clear exactly what they're working to achieve.

Option 3: This option is incorrect. Just giving the team members more challenging sales targets won't make them think of their work or the organization more positively. Unless they're given more of a sense of purpose and inspired to achieve broader, organizational goals, it's also unlikely that their performance will improve.

Option 4: This option is correct. The manager can help promote a more positive culture by leading in a way that inspires the team members to follow her example. In this case, her optimism is likely to be infectious.

Option 5: This is a correct option. The manager can foster a more positive workplace culture by demonstrating qualities like honesty and integrity. This will encourage members of the team to respect her and to be inspired by her example. In turn, they're likely to feel more positive about their jobs.

Managers can help develop a sense of belonging in employees by always emphasizing that everyone is part of the same team. This involves making it clear that all employees and managers are working toward common goals and making sure employees know these goals.

For example, managers can always refer to both themselves and employees as "we" or "us."

Leaders should also help unite employees around company goals by highlighting external threats such as competition. However, the aim isn't to make employees feel insecure. It's to stress that everyone needs to work together to overcome threats and to help the organization succeed.

They can also regularly invite employees to contribute their own ideas and feedback. Employees generally have a more positive outlook if they feel that they're active participants in an organization's decisions, and in its successes or failures.

An organization can help cultivate a sense of belonging among employees through social activities and functions that are consistent with its shared values. For example, team-building exercises or company outings can encourage employees to bond socially and build comradery. An organization that operates internationally might hold a conference over several days and encourage employees to socialize in the evenings.

Question

How can you develop a sense of belonging and oneness in an organization?

Options:

1. When you address the employees, you can refer to everyone as "we" and "us"

2. You can introduce team building exercises and occasional outings

3. You can invite the employees to share their input with different projects

4. You can detail the threats the company is facing and the competition it has to overcome

5. When addressing the employees, you can make sure they understand the consequences of not performing

6. You can create a progress chart that rates the employees against each other to encourage them to perform

Answer

You can develop a sense of belonging and oneness by referring to employees as "we" and "us," introducing team building exercises, detailing the threats the company needs to overcome, and inviting the employees to share their input.

As well as developing a sense of belonging, you can help cultivate a positive workplace culture by developing a sense of history in employees. Explaining an organization's background and how much it has achieved can motivate employees and make them feel more secure. You can develop a sense of history by talking about the heroes of the company's past and their contributions, and by developing rituals and ceremonies.

Heroes of the past

Employees can use the knowledge of how company heroes of the past made their achievements, and the knowledge of what attempts failed and why, to create new and innovative solutions for achieving organizational goals.

If employees understand how previous organizational goals were met, they will have a better idea of how to meet the current goals. This helps employees succeed in their work and adapt to company culture, promoting a sense of positivity.

Rituals and ceremonies

You can add to employees' sense of history by developing various rituals and traditions. For example, your organization might reserve the same day every year – the day it was founded, for example – for a company outing. Or it may mark the successful close of each project with a small ceremony where the project manager makes a speech and then everyone has cake and coffee.

Ceremonies, like celebrating employees' birthdays, can also help make employees feel valued and recognized.

You can provide employees with a sense of history by showing a video or slide show that details how the company began, and how it got to its current position. For example, a large chain of restaurants can teach the employees how the chain began with one man's desire to share his love of food with others. This will encourage employees to feel a sense of pride and positivity in working toward their company's future success.

The decisions and strategies the company used to expand and become successful can then be shared with the employees. These ideas that led to success will inspire employees to come up with their own ideas to achieve success.

Employee satisfaction and diversity

A fourth way to help build a positive culture in the workplace is to focus on improving employees' satisfaction. Employees who like their jobs are more productive and perform to higher standards than those who don't. To boost employees' job satisfaction, you can provide employees with emotional support, show concern for individuals, make a commitment to understand your employees' needs, and help employees progress in their careers.

Provide emotional support

As well as providing employees with work-related support, you should provide them with a certain amount of emotional support.

For example, employees may have personal problems or experience various types of trauma outside work, and this can affect their performance at work. As a good manager, you don't need to help with employees' personal issues, but you should provide understanding and acknowledge the difficulties they're experiencing.

You can also provide employees with emotional support if they're feeling uncertain about their work or overwhelmed. For example, you can reassure new employees that they're doing fine and that you're there to support them.

Show concern for individuals

You can help improve employees' job satisfaction by making them feel valued and supported, and by demonstrating that you care about their well-being. If an employee's work is being affected by an external crisis, you should acknowledge that it isn't the employee's fault.

Understand employees' needs

If you're to help ensure the happiness of employees in their jobs, you need to understand their individual needs and aspirations. Then you can take steps to satisfy these.

For example, you can delegate more challenging tasks to employees who feel under-challenged.

Help employees progress

Employees generally feel more positive if they believe they're progressing in their careers. So as a manager, you can promote a more positive culture by taking an active interest in employees' career goals.

You can encourage employees to formulate career goals for themselves. If they see their current work as a means of acquiring experience and skills, and of advancing in their careers, they're likely to be more motivated and productive.

You can also help employees achieve particular goals by assisting them in developing relevant skills – for example, by assigning them tasks where they can learn new skills, or having them attend relevant training.

Question

The sales manager at the computer company has decided she needs to improve employee satisfaction because of low morale and complaints of boredom.

How can she improve employee satisfaction?

Options:

1. She can have private meetings with employees to give them a chance to share their feelings, and do her best to support them

2. She can identify individuals who are struggling and show concern for their success

3. She can hold a team meeting and encourage team members to share their needs

4. She can provide employees with more challenges to keep their work interesting

5. She can compare the team's progress with other teams to stress the need to improve

6. She can tell the members of the team that if things don't improve, she may have to implement pay cuts

Answer

To improve employee satisfaction, the sales manager can provide the employees with emotional support, show concern for individuals, understand the employees' needs, and help them progress in their careers.

A final strategy for cultivating a positive culture among employees is to foster diversity. An organization has a diverse workforce if it employs people with a wide range of differences.

Diversity doesn't relate just to cultural background or ethnicity. It also relates to characteristics like gender, age, training, work style, and status.

For organizations, encouraging diversity can have several benefits:

- being able to adapt quickly and easily to changes and new situations, because of the diverse experiences and knowledge of employees,
- displaying higher levels of innovation, as a result of access to different perspectives and ways of thinking,
- improving the company's ability to operate internationally, with employees having different languages and knowledge of different cultures, and
- generating improved employee performance, as a result of all employees feeling respected regardless of their individual differences.

To foster diversity in the workplace, you should develop your own knowledge, and identify and overcome your own biases. You should also validate employees' varying perspectives, encourage integrity, recognize and prohibit unacceptable behavior, show a willingness to change, and demonstrate the strategic value of diversity.

Develop your knowledge

The first thing you can do to help foster diversity is to learn more about it. You can read newsletters, leaflets, and any other publications available, and attend seminars. This will help you learn more about the benefits of diversity and how to manage it. You can also learn from mistakes other organizations have made.

Identify own biases

It's important to identify your own biases so you can make an effort to overcome them. Otherwise stereotypes and distorted perceptions can prevent you from managing diversity properly.

Validate varying perspectives

To help foster diversity, you need to make it clear that different perspectives and ideas are welcomed. You might not agree with certain points of view, but every employee should have a right to their own opinions – and it's important to encourage them to express these.

Exercise integrity and ethics

By making decisions that are ethically sound and always behaving fairly, you can encourage employees to follow suit. This overcomes cultural barriers and helps ensure all employees treat one another with respect.

Prohibit unacceptable behavior

It's vital to recognize and prohibit behavior that involves discriminating against others because of their backgrounds or personal characteristics. You should deal with this type of behavior immediately, making it clear that it won't be tolerated.

For example, if an employee makes offensive jokes about another person's culture or race, it's vital to discipline the employee.

Show willingness to change

You can help foster diversity by demonstrating a willingness and openness to change. This can help others to accept differences and to realize the potential benefits of embracing diversity.

Demonstrate strategic value

Managers can manage diversity strategically, ensuring it contributes to an organization's ability to gain a competitive edge. For example, a diverse workforce tends to be more innovative than one that's fairly heterogeneous. A manager can capitalize on this to help an organization achieve its business goals and overtake competitors.

Case Study: Question 1 of 2
Scenario

Neil and Polly work as managers for a recruitment company. Neil manages a division that handles all recruitment for a major bank. In the division, employees' use of sick leave has greatly increased over the last few months and many employees have started arriving at work late. In interviews, some employees express frustration. They feel they can't express their opinions and also don't know what they're working toward.

Polly manages a department that recruits candidates for temporary positions. In her department, some employees are becoming sloppy in their work. Employees don't feel valued, so turnover is high. The environment is highly competitive.

Answer the questions in any order to determine how the department managers can promote a more positive workplace culture in their organization.

Question

What can Neil do to help create a positive culture?

Options:

1. Neil can provide the employees with a full background of the company and how it has come to succeed over the years

2. Neil can give the employees the right to express their opinions, even if he may not agree with all of them

3. Neil can find out where these rumors are coming from and stop them from spreading

4. Neil can introduce a disciplinary system so that employees will feel they need to perform better

Answer

Option 1: This is a correct option. A manager can promote a positive culture by developing a sense of history. The employees will gain a better understanding of the company's organizational goals by knowing where the company came from.

Option 2: This option is correct. Neil can cultivate a positive culture by fostering diversity. By taking into account all the employees' different views and experiences, innovative solutions can be found. First Neil has to identify his own biases in order to make sure they don't affect his work.

Option 3: This is an incorrect option. Stopping so-called rumors won't help promote positivity in the workplace. Neil should instead foster diversity and listen to the employees' views. He can also cultivate a positive culture by developing a sense of history so that employees can get a better understanding of the company's direction.

Option 4: This option is incorrect. Threatening the employees will not help cultivate a positive culture in the workplace. Neil can promote a positive culture by fostering diversity and developing a sense of history so that employees' will have a better understanding of how the company works.

Case Study: Question 2 of 2

What can Polly do to cultivate a positive culture?

Options:

1. She can lead by example, always demonstrating enthusiasm and reminding employees of good things about working for the company

2. She can make an effort to understand and cater to employees' needs, and provide appropriate emotional support

3. She can explain external threats to the company and the need to work together

4. She can discipline employees who demonstrate negative behavior and attitudes 5. She can give the employees more challenging deadlines

Answer

Option 1: This is a correct option. Polly can help cultivate a positive culture in the workplace by influencing the employees through her leadership. She can lead in a way that will make employees want to mirror her behavior – for example, by remaining positive and showing enthusiasm.

Option 2: This option is correct. Polly can focus on employee satisfaction to help create a positive environment. She can do this by making a commitment to understand all the employees, and by providing them with emotional support.

Option 3: This is a correct option. Polly can develop a sense of unity among employees to cultivate a positive culture. One way to do this is to emphasize that they're all working together to overcome external threats.

Option 4: This option is incorrect. Disciplining employees will only make them more negative. Instead, Polly should influence the employees through her leadership, focus on employee satisfaction, and create a sense of unity so that employees work together.

Option 5: This is an incorrect option. Giving more challenging deadlines won't necessarily meet employees' needs. Instead Polly should influence the employees through her leadership, make the employees feel like they're valued, focus on employee satisfaction, and develop a sense of unity by encouraging employees to work together.

REFERENCES

References
1. **Organizational Behavior, 11th Edition** - 2010, John R. Schermerhorn, Jr., James G. Hunt, Richard N. Osborn and Mary Uhl-Bien, John Wiley & Sons
2. **Managing Organizational Behavior** - 2002, Ronald R. Sims, Quorum Books
3. **Organization Behaviour for Leisure Services** - 2003, Conrad Lashley and Darren Lee-Ross, Butterworth-Heinemann
4. **The Manager as Politician** - 2005, Jerry W. Gilley, Greenwood Press
5. **Smart Management: Using Politics in Organisations** - 2001, David Butcher and Martin Clarke, Palgrave Macmillan